Costume Jewellery

JUDITH MILLER

DK

LONDON, NEW YORK,
MUNICH, MELBOURNE, DELHI

A joint production from DK and THE PRICE GUIDE COMPANY

DK DELHI
Editors Saloni Talwar, Pankhoori Sinha
Designers Shefali Upadhyay, Romi Chakraborty
DTP Designers Pankaj Sharma, Harish Aggarwal, Pushpak Tyagi **Cutouts** Neeraj Aggarwal
Manager Aparna Sharma

DK LONDON
Senior Editor Janet Mohun
Designer Katie Eke
Production Editor Vania Cunha
Production Inderjit Bhullar
Managing Art Editor Christine Keilty

THE PRICE GUIDE COMPANY LIMITED
[illegible]
Editorial Assistant [illegible]
Workflow consultant [illegible] **Photographer** [illegible]

While every care has been taken in the compilation of this guide, neither the authors nor the publishers accept any liability for any financial or other loss incurred by reliance placed on the information contained in *Costume Jewelry.*

[illegible]

CIP catalog records for this book are available from the Library of Congress and the British Library.

US ISBN-978-0-7566-2619-8
UK ISBN-978-1-4053-1812-9

Proofing by MDP, UK
Printed in China by Hung Hing Offset Printing Company Ltd

Discover more at
www.dk.com

CONTENTS

INTRODUCTION

Whether it's sparkling with hundreds of diamanté stones or glistening with crystals and pearls, there's nothing like a piece of costume jewelry to turn heads. In recent years many of us have fallen in love with its glamour and glitz. Vintage pieces are beautiful reminders of the styles of yesterday – a 1940s Trifari pin looks as good on a lapel today as it did way back when. From colorful Bakelite to demure faux pearls there's something for everyone and so much to choose from. So indulge yourself with a glittering treasure or two – you'll be in good company!

Judith Miller

Star Ratings

Each of the costume jewelry pieces in this book has a star rating according to its value:

★ $50–100; £25–50 ★★ $100–300; £50–150 ★★★ $300–500; £150–250

★★★★ $500–1000; £250–500 ★★★★★ $1,000 upward; £500 upward

GOLDEN ERA DESIGNERS

Celebrity parties, fashion catwalks, Oscar ceremonies, and the fashionable parts of town: it is almost impossible to escape the craze for vintage costume jewelry. The concept of nonprecious "costume" jewelry dates back to ancient civilizations when people adorned themselves with decorative but readily available objects. Over the centuries, advancements in materials led to a greater diversity of affordable styles. The mid-20th century was a boom time for designers. Chanel and Schiaparelli led the way by introducing radical style ideas, while Hollywood stars (such as Pier Angeli, left) became influential fashion icons. Following the end of World War II, the design world left behind austerity and embraced the glamour and frivolity of Dior, Haskell, and many other talented individuals. Leading designers from this 20th century "Golden Age" created costume jewelry that became not only as desirable and innovative as precious jewelry, but also as sought after today as it was in its Golden Era.

CHANEL

Coco Chanel (1883–1971) revolutionized fashion and inspired designers throughout the 20th century. Her chic yet practical suits and understated accessories appealed to women enjoying the new-found freedom of the 1920s. Dedicating a salon in her Parisian boutique to accessories, Chanel designed stylish jewelry that complemented the simple lines and colors of her clothes, rather than copying the fine jewelry of the period. Elegance and simplicity were the hallmarks of her work, offset by showy pearls that became a trend for fashion-conscious women. Affordable materials such as faux pearls, gold-tone chains, and poured glass were used alongside precious materials in pieces designed by her. Today, an original box can increase the value of Chanel pieces by up to 30 percent.

Rare Chanel star pin, in gold-plated metal. *1930s* ★★★★★

Pair of floral motif earrings of gold-plated metal with red glass cabochon centers and petals of green poured glass and clear crystal rhinestones. *1980s* ★★★★☆

Floral motif with bow pin of green, blue, and red poured glass, pink and amethyst beads, clear rhinestones, and faux pearls set in gilt metal. *1930s* ★★★☆☆

"The best color in the whole world is one that looks good on you!"

Coco Chanel

Bijoux de Fleurs orchid pin in shades of pink and red enameled pot metal with smokey brown crystal rhinestones. *Late 1920s* ★★★★

Stylized floral pin with green, red, and blue poured glass stones, faux pearls, and pavé-set clear crystal rhinestones. *1920s* ★★★★

In the 1920s and 30s, Chanel retailed a series of novelty and creature pins made from enameled cast lead.

Rare Mr Punch pin with an *en tremblant* head in lead with white, red, and black enamel. The head is set with crystal rhinestones. *1920s* ★★★★★

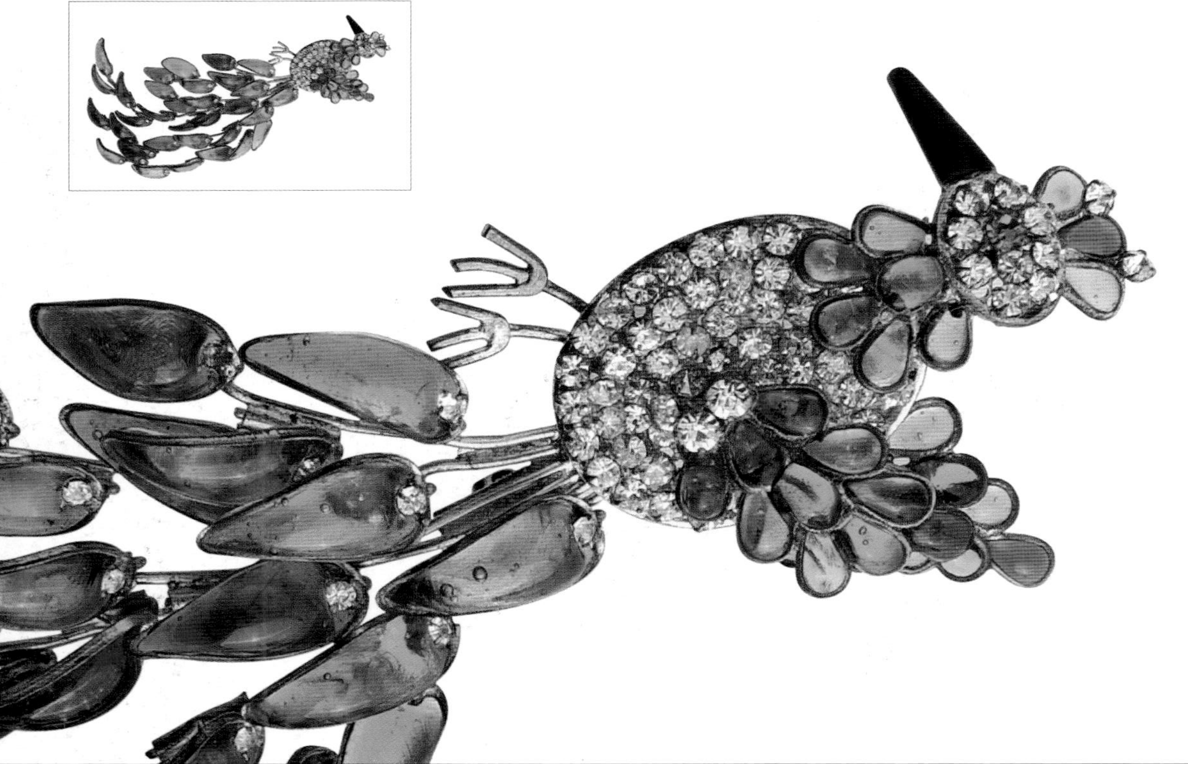

Rare peacock pin with turquoise, aquamarine, and red poured glass feathers and pavé-set clear crystal rhinestones. *1930s* ★★★★★

French couture bracelet with poured ruby red glass set in gilded metal. *1950s* ★★★★★

"How many cares one loses when one decides not to be something but to be someone."

Coco Chanel

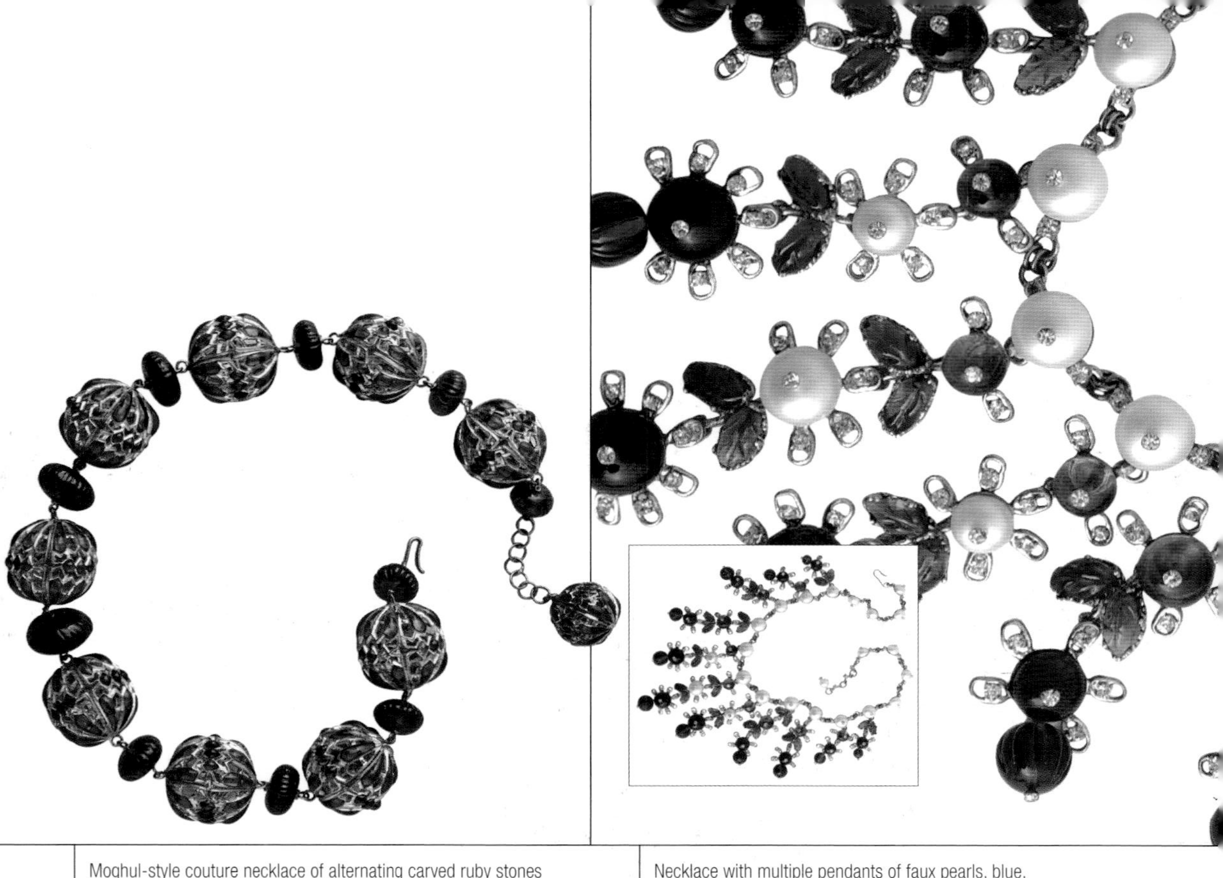

Moghul-style couture necklace of alternating carved ruby stones and emerald glass beads encased in filigree gilt metal with ruby glass highlights. *1950s* ★★★★★

Necklace with multiple pendants of faux pearls, blue, red, and green poured glass beads, and clear crystal rhinestones. *c.1970* ★★★★★

CORO

Employing nearly 3,500 staff during the height of production in the 1930s and 40s, Coro became a leading name in American costume jewelry. The prolific output meant that styles were produced at every quality level and for every budget. Although not officially incorporated as Coro until 1943, the company was founded in 1901. From the mid-1920s, Coro expanded rapidly under the guidance of design director Adolph Katz. The talented designer was responsible for a number of hugely successful pieces, including his *en tremblant* floral pins (in which a motif is mounted on a spring so that it trembles when the wearer moves), Jelly Bellies, and Coro Duettes. Other important designers included Gene Verecchio and Albert Weiss. Pieces marked "Coro" tended to be of good quality while the Corocraft range targeted the higher end of the market.

Coro plume pin with emerald green glass stones and clear crystal rhinestone highlights on a gold-plated frame. *1940s* ★★★☆☆

Corocraft diamanté, glass, and faux pearl lovebirds pin. *1940s* ★★☆☆☆

Large Corocraft pin of scrolling forms and stylized floral motif in sterling silver set with ruby glass cabochons and round-cut crystal rhinestones. *Mid-1940s* ★★☆☆☆

Floral Coro Duette in gold wash on white metal set with green crystal baguettes and clear crystal rhinestones. *1940s* ★★★☆☆

"For me, elegance is not to pass unnoticed but to get to the very soul of what one is."

Christian Lacroix

Coro Duette parrots in yellow metal with green, blue, and pink enameling and pavé-set clear crystal rhinestones. *1940s* ★★☆☆☆

Coro Duette owl pins, with blue enamel and large aquamarine and clear crystal rhinestones over a sterling-silver casting. *Mid-1940s* ★★★☆☆

Coro Duette pin with crowns in vermeil sterling silver with ruby and emerald crystal rhinestones and faux pearls. *1940s* ★★★☆☆

Pair of Coro "his and hers" penguin pins in enameled pot metal with pink cabochons and diamanté accents. ★★☆☆☆

The materials used and the current appreciation of particular styles ultimately determine the price of Coro pieces.

Very rare Coro Duette "brave and squaw" pin in vermeil sterling silver with red and green enamel, and ruby and clear crystal rhinestones. *1940s* ★★★★★

Coro Duette bouquets of flowers in enameled silver with red glass beads and clear crystal rhinestones. The bouquets can be separated and worn individually. *1930s* ★★☆☆☆

Corocraft is the best known of Coro's upmarket brands.

Gold-plated bracelet by Corocraft set with faux ruby cabochons, green enamel, and pavé crystal rhinestones. *1940s* ★★★★★

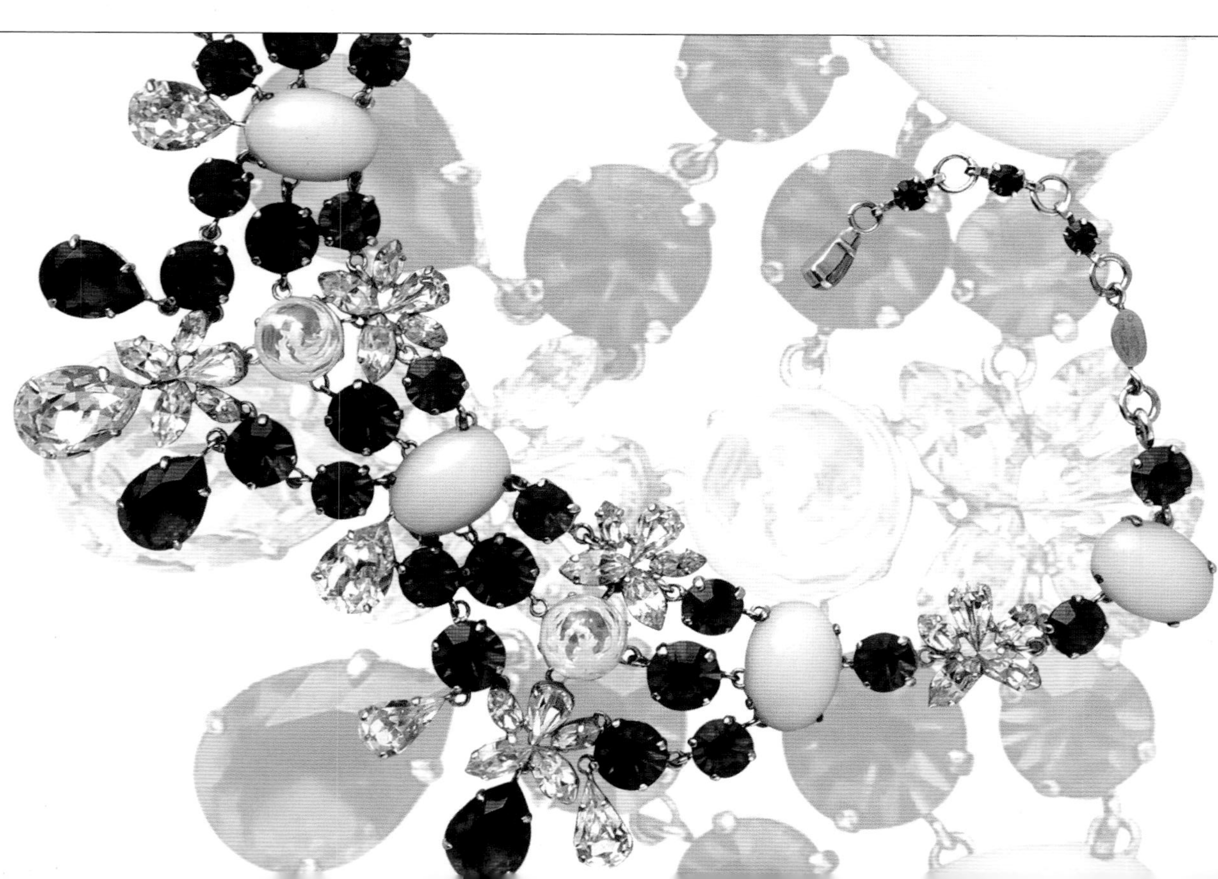

CHRISTIAN DIOR

Internationally renowned for introducing the extravagant and ultra-feminine "New Look" style following the austerity of World War II, Christian Dior (1905–57) dominated the world of fashion during the 1940s and 50s. Costume jewelry was designed as an integral part of his *haute couture* collections. Early pieces were almost exclusively made for wealthy and high-profile clients such as Bette Davis, while later examples were made under license in far greater numbers. Keen to maintain high standards, the House of Dior commissioned many important designers, including Henry Schreiner, Mitchell Maer, and Josette Gripoix. In the years following Dior's death, great names in fashion such as Yves Saint Laurent have also designed for the company. Floral motifs, *aurora borealis* rhinestones, and unusual, high-quality stones are typical of Dior.

Christian Dior necklace and earrings set with white, clear, and red paste stones. *1959* ★★★★★

Mitchell Maer was licensed to produce jewelry for Dior in 1952. His unicorn pins are much sought-after by collectors.

Mitchell Maer for Dior unicorn pin of rhodium-plated metal with pavé-set clear rhinestones. *Mid-1950s* ★★☆☆☆

Rare bird pin in sterling silver, enamel, faux pearls, and paste with *en tremblant* wings. *1958* ★★★★★

Rare snail on a leaf pin in sterling silver and paste. *c.1958* ★★★★★

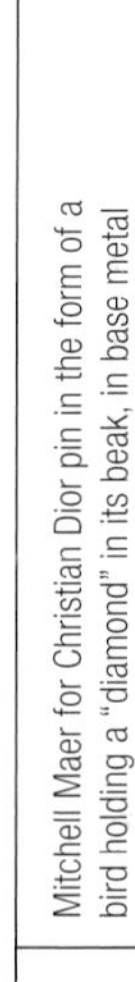

Mitchell Maer for Christian Dior pin in the form of a bird holding a "diamond" in its beak, in base metal and paste. *1950–52* ★★★★★

Stylized fruit pin with faux sapphires, rubies, diamonds, and pearls. *1962* ★★★★☆

German company Henkel and Grosse was selected to manufacture jewelry for Dior in 1955.

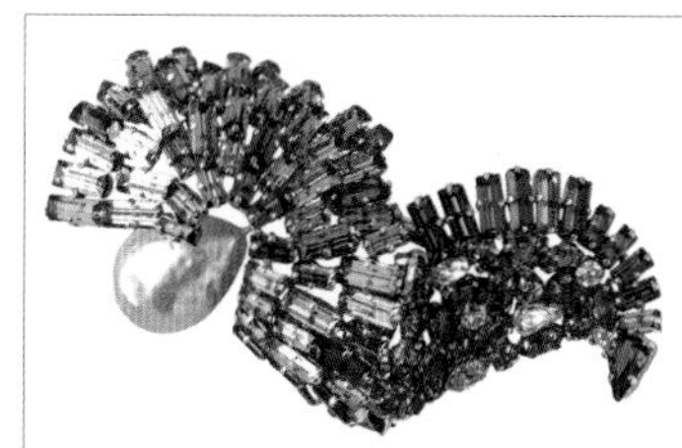

Henkel and Grosse pin for Dior, of white metal set with emerald, amethyst, and clear rhinestone baguettes, and a faux pearl. *1962* ★★★★☆

Rhodium-plated floral necklace and earrings with round- and navette-cut faux rubies and clear rhinestones. *1959* ★★★★☆

"Zest is the secret of all beauty. There is no beauty that is attractive without zest."

Christian Dior

Gold-plated floral necklace with faux pearls, prong-set red cabochons and topaz, and emerald green rhinestones. *1958* ★★☆☆☆

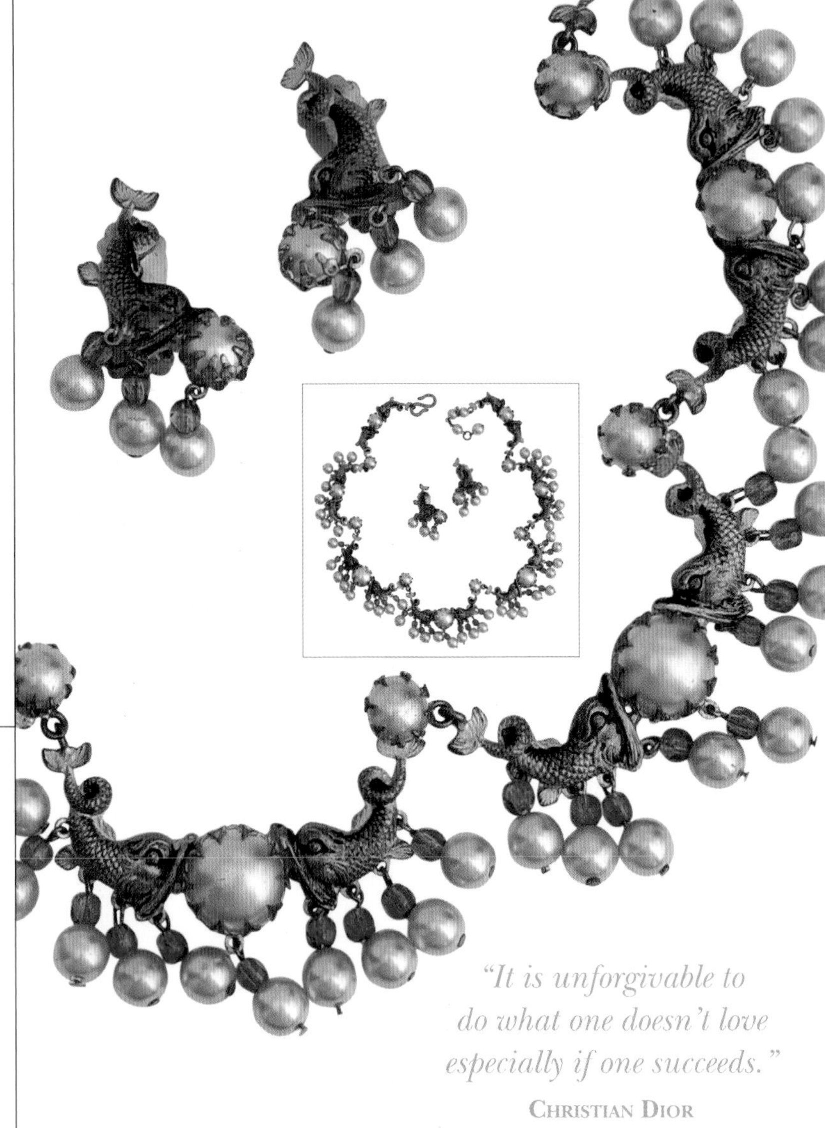

Extremely rare necklace and earrings, consisting of gilded metal mythical sea creatures and set with faux pearls and green glass. *1959* ★★★★★

"It is unforgivable to do what one doesn't love especially if one succeeds."

CHRISTIAN DIOR

The opulence of the groundbreaking "New Look" collection of 1947 was sustained by the House of Dior during the late 1950s and 60s.

Pendant necklace and earrings of gilt metal with rectangular-cut jonquil pastes, black enamel cabochons, faux pearls, and clear rhinestones. *1963* ★★★★★

BIRDS

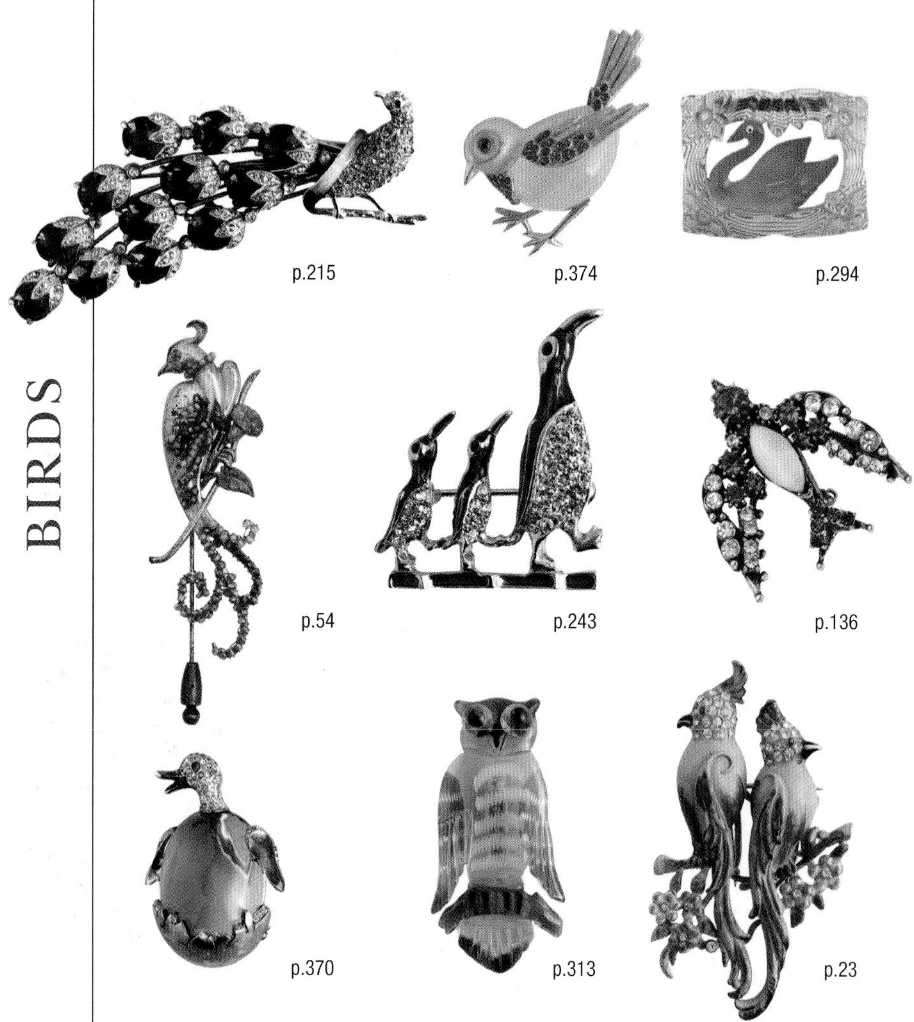

p.215
p.374
p.294
p.54
p.243
p.136
p.370
p.313
p.23

p.24 p.112 p.162

p.225 p.369

p.241 p.312 p.15

JOSEFF OF HOLLYWOOD

Showcased in classic movies such as *Gone with the Wind, Cleopatra*, and *Breakfast at Tiffany's,* Eugene Joseff's jewelry evokes the glamour of Hollywood and is highly desirable today. After abandoning a career in advertising to pursue his passion, Joseff (1905–48) became a leading supplier of costume jewelry to major film studios. As well as developing a matt, camera-friendly alternative to gold known as Russian gold, Joseff had the skills to research and simplify historical styles to convey an era on screen. Typical objects include pins, pendants, and earrings in styles as diverse as Art Deco and Middle-Eastern. Most pieces are stamped with the company name, except one-off examples, which are often unsigned. Some early pieces have been reissued in recent years and, although sought-after, these are slightly less valuable.

Sun god pin in Russian gold with clear rhinestone eye tremblers; one of Joseff's most distinctive pieces. *1940s* ★★★☆

Very rare silver and red Bakelite leaf pin. *1940s* ★★☆☆☆

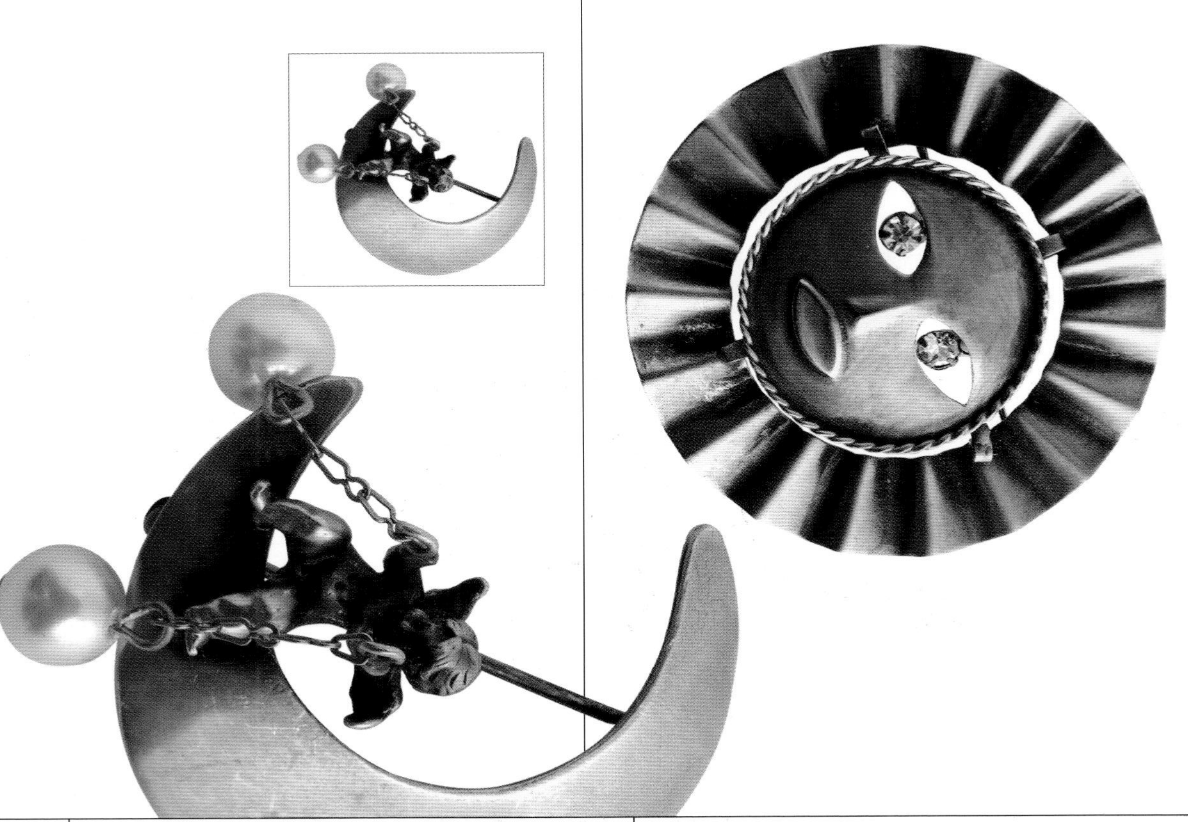

Crescent moon pin with cherub and pearl charms. ★★☆☆☆

Very rare Russian gold-plated Moon god with ruff pin, with clear rhinestone eye tremblers. *1940s* ★★★★☆

Large Russian gold-plated tassel pin of Middle-Eastern inspiration, with faux silver finish. *1940s* ★★★★☆

Joseff of Hollywood "Joseff" retail display logo, Russian gold-plated. *1930s–50s* ★★☆☆☆

Gold-colored flowerhead with bees pins. *1940s* ★★★☆☆

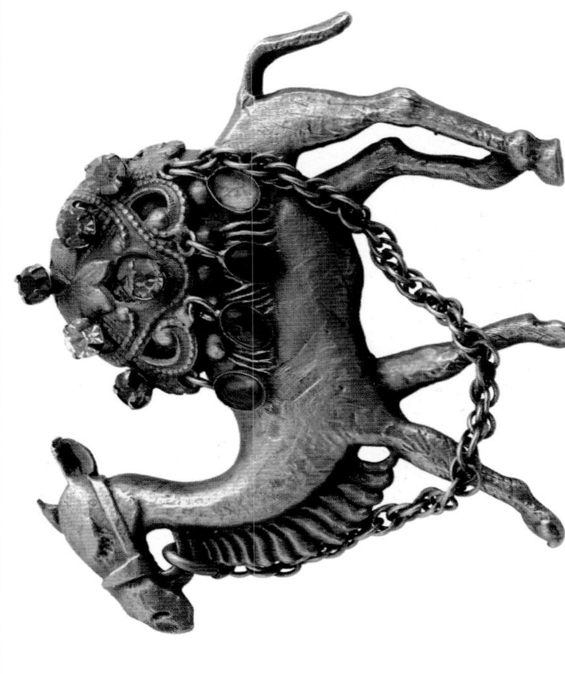

Russian gold-plated pair-of-wolves pin with ruby, chalcedony, amber, and sapphire crystal cabochons. *1940s* ★★☆☆☆

Russian gold-plated châtelaine camel pin with ruby, emerald, citrine, jade, and aquamarine crystal cabochons. *1940s* ★★★★☆

Collection of Russian gold-plated bee pins of varying sizes. *1940s* ★☆☆☆☆

Russian gold-plated American eagle and flag pin, with prong-set ruby, sapphire, and clear rhinestones. *1940s* ★★☆☆☆

Unusual Russian gold-plated floral motif necklace and earrings with navette-cut ruby and round-cut clear rhinestones. *1940s* ★★★★★

Joseff was critical of the use of historically incorrect jewelry in Hollywood movies and so began designing more authentic pieces of his own.

"Beauty is not caused. It is."

Emily Dickinson

Russian gold-plated floral motif pendant necklace and earrings, with faux topaz and clear rhinestones. *1940s* ★★★★★

MIRIAM HASKELL

Miriam Haskell (1899–1981) played a key role in elevating the status of costume jewelry from inexpensive copies of precious pieces to a fashionable and valuable accessory in its own right. Haskell opened her first jewelry shop in New York in 1924 and, although she was not a designer herself, she developed a talent for spotting the potential of the creative people she employed and choosing which of their designs to put into production. Her designs were so successful and innovative that they were widely imitated. She guided the company to great success and established a star-studded client list. Her designers used materials of high quality, including beads from Murano, Italy and faceted glass crystals from Austria.

Two-strand necklace of faux black pearls with a flower pendant made of faux black pearl disks, rose montées, and gilded brass leaves, all hand-wired onto a gilded brass filigree backing. *1950s* ★★★☆

Flower and leaf pin of antiqued gilt metal with melon-cut emerald beads and clear rose montées. *c.1960* ★★★★☆

Hollywood actress Joan Crawford regularly bought Haskell jewelry from the early 1930s to the late 1960s. Her extensive collection was auctioned amid much publicity in 1978.

Pair of earrings set with green glass pumpkin-cut beads, amber beads, and faux pearls. *1950s* ★★☆☆☆

Bird of paradise on a branch stick pin made of antiqued gilt metal with sapphire, emerald, and pink glass beads. *1940s* ★★☆☆☆

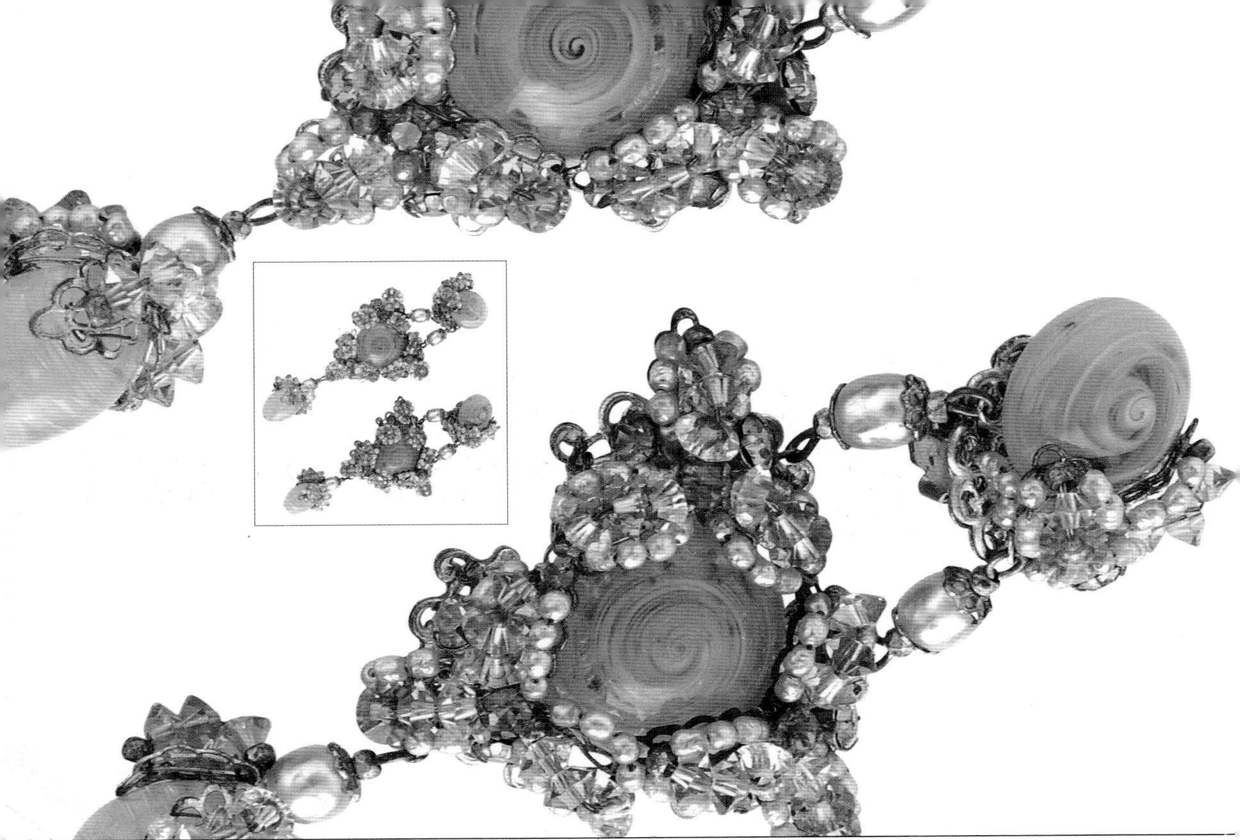

Pair of earrings with long drops holding pink glass stones surrounded by clusters of pastel stones. *1950s* ★★★★☆

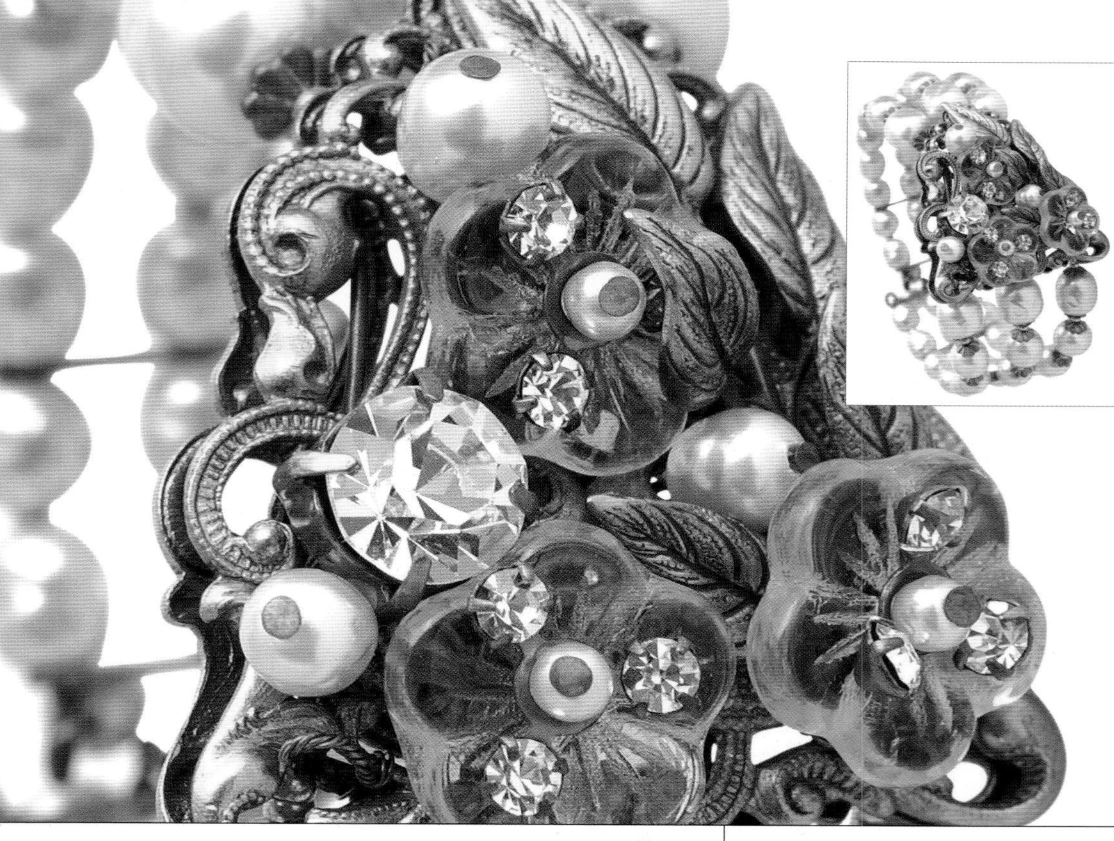

Three-strand graduated faux pearl clamper bracelet decorated with peridot glass flowers and crystal highlights. *1950s* ★★★☆☆

Clamper bracelet made of gilded brass with leaves and filigree flowers set with faux pearls and seed pearls. *1950s* ★★☆☆☆

Floral necklace and earrings with amber, pear-cut glass cabochons, citrine glass oval beads, and citrine and amber rhinestones. *c.1950* ★★★★★

Haskell jewelry has often appeared in theater, film, and television, in shows such as The Phantom of the Opera *and* I Love Lucy.

Shooting star necklace with strands of baroque pearls and a pendant with two ears of wheat in gilded metal set with rose montées, and tassels of pearls with oblong faux pearl pendants. *c.1963* ★★★★

Two-strand necklace of graduated faux pearls with a flower pendant of faux pearl disks and diamanté and brass flowers, on a gilded brass filigree backing. *1950s* ★★★★☆

Miriam Haskell necklace with multiple-beaded discs and pearl drops. *1940s* ★★★★

SCHIAPARELLI

Elsa Schiaparelli's (1890–1973) exuberant, cutting-edge designs set the fashion world alight, and shocked critics during the 1930s. The Italian-born fashion designer was known for her outrageous and witty clothing that was inspired by modern and Surrealist art, and for her use of new materials such as cellophane and zippers. She saw jewelry as an essential element in creating a "look" and produced a wide range of quirky pieces that drew inspiration from exotic flora, circus imagery, and astrological motifs. In 1936, Schiaparelli introduced a range of jewelry in her signature "shocking pink" color. Abstract and floral glass pieces from the 1940s and 50s are easier to come by than the rare 1930s examples.

Necklace and earrings with lava rock cabochons and *aurora borealis* crystals. *1950s* ★★★★☆

Speckled blue glass and faux pearl pin. ★★☆☆☆

Gold-plated frog on a leaf pin. The frog has a dark blue cabochon body, ruby red, kite-shaped glass feet, and faux pearl eyes. *1950s* ★★★☆☆

"Fashion is born by small facts, trends, or even politics, never by trying to make little pleats and furbelows, by trinkets, by clothes easy to copy, or by the shortening or lengthening of a skirt."

ELSA SCHIAPARELLI

Yellow metal acorn and leaf earrings set with *aurora borealis* stones. ★★☆☆☆

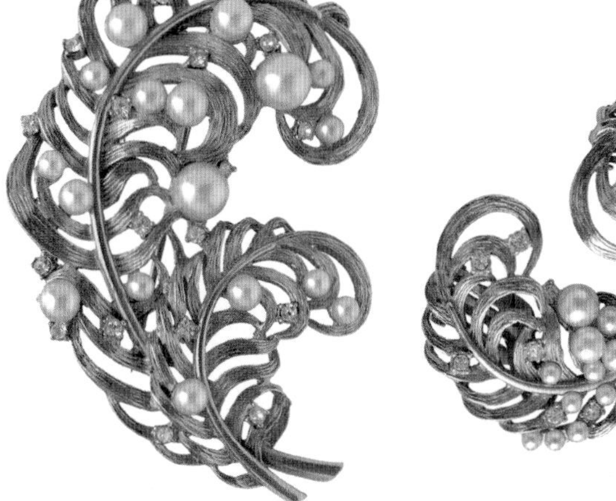

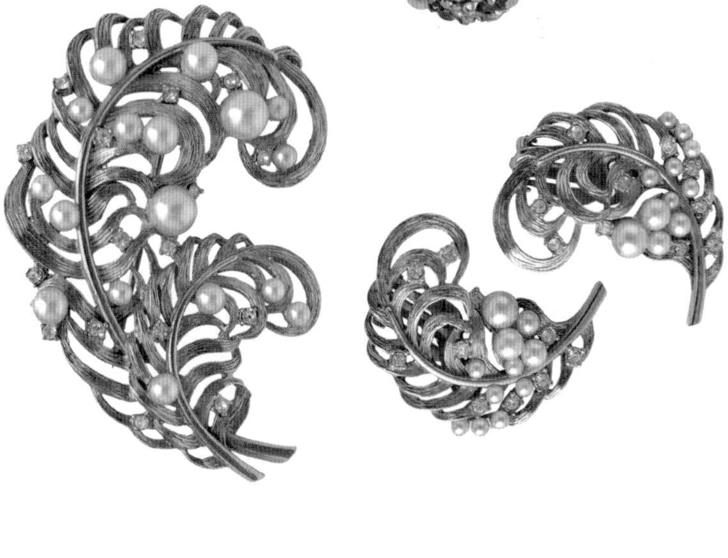

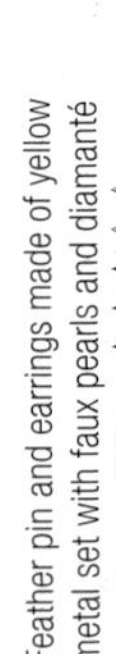

Feather pin and earrings made of yellow metal set with faux pearls and diamanté accents. *1950s* ★★★☆☆

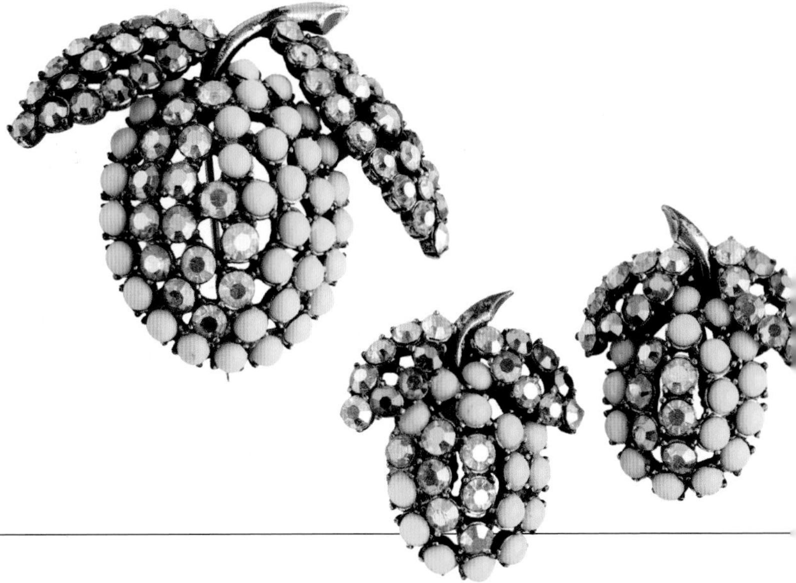

Fruit pin and earrings, with a mixture of *aurora borealis* stones and yellow Bakelite cabochons. *1950s* ★★★★☆

Earrings with carved rose stones surrounded by red *aurora borealis* navette stones and clear *aurora borealis* stones set in gun metal-plated casting. *1950s* ★★☆☆☆

Flora and fauna were recurring themes in Schiaparelli's designs.

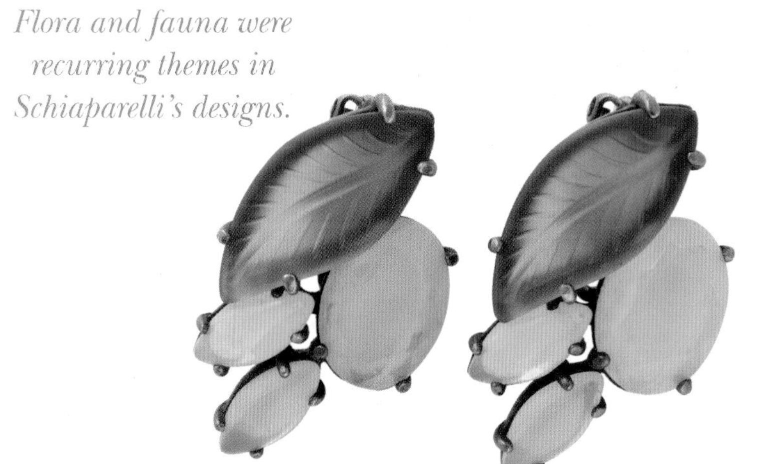

Pair of brown and green moonstone leaf earrings. *1950s* ★★☆☆☆

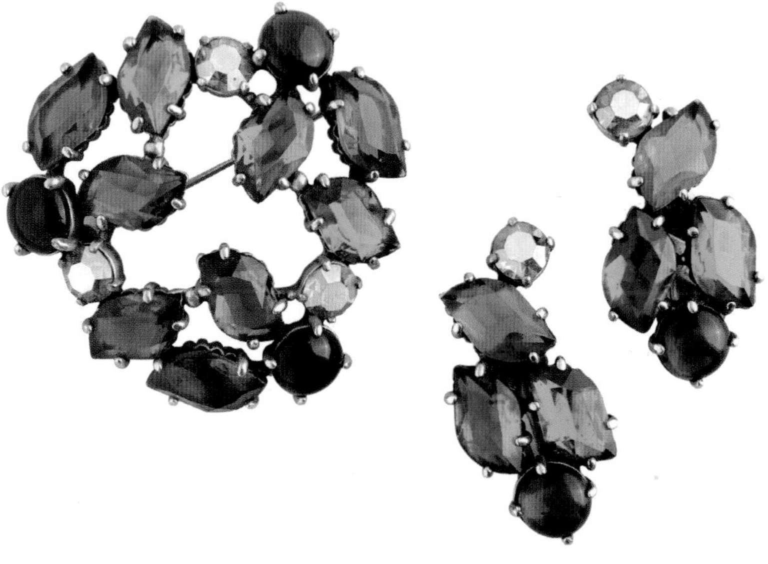

Pin and earrings with prong-set blue cabochons and blue and green crystal rhinestones. *1950s* ★★★☆☆

Pin and earrings with textured amethyst cabochons and crystals. ★★★☆☆

Bracelet and earrings with iridescent blue and *aurora borealis* stones. *1950s* ★★★☆☆

"We ascribe beauty to that which is simple; which has no superfluous parts; which exactly answers its end; which stands related to all things; which is the mean of many extremes."

RALPH WALDO EMERSON

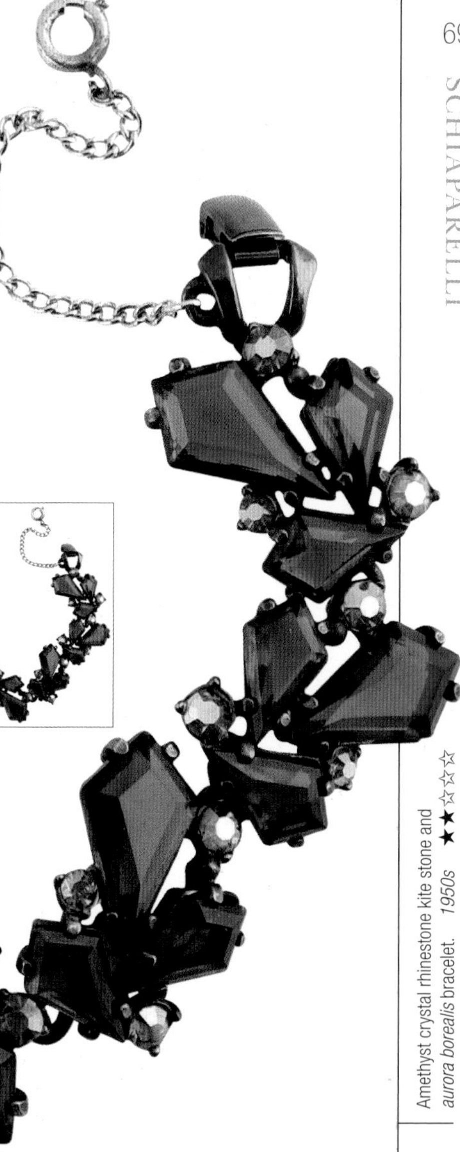

Amethyst crystal rhinestone kite stone and *aurora borealis* bracelet. *1950s* ★★☆☆☆

Bracelet, brooch, and earrings with faux emeralds in a gilt metal setting. *1950s* ★★★★☆

"In difficult times fashion is always outrageous."

Elsa Schiaparelli

Bracelet, brooch, and earrings set with *aurora borealis* stones and faux pearls. *1950s* ★★★☆☆

p.228 p.306 p.174
p.228 p.307 p.160
p.25 p.151 p.204

p.208  p.42  p.211

p.240  p.24  p.314

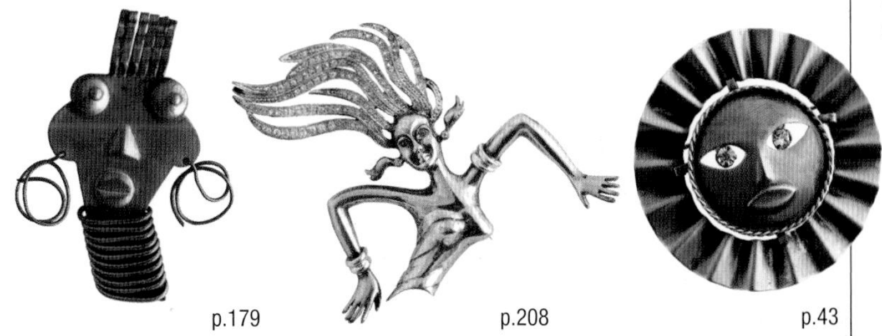

p.179 p.208 p.43

STANLEY HAGLER

American designer Stanley Hagler (1923–96) was known for his bold, colorful, and seemingly larger than life designs. After working briefly as an advisor to Miriam Haskell in the late 1940s, Hagler began to create his own jewelry designs. Working in glass, stone, and crystals, Hagler specialized in faux pearls that were made from hand-blown glass dipped in pearl resin up to 15 times. Inspiration came from contemporary designs as well as antique jewelry. Quality was high, winning him the loyal following of celebrity clients such as Wallis Simpson, the Duchess of Windsor. Pieces were typically wired by hand and crystals were prong-set rather than glued. Many pieces were three-dimensional in appearance, making them visually appealing from all angles.

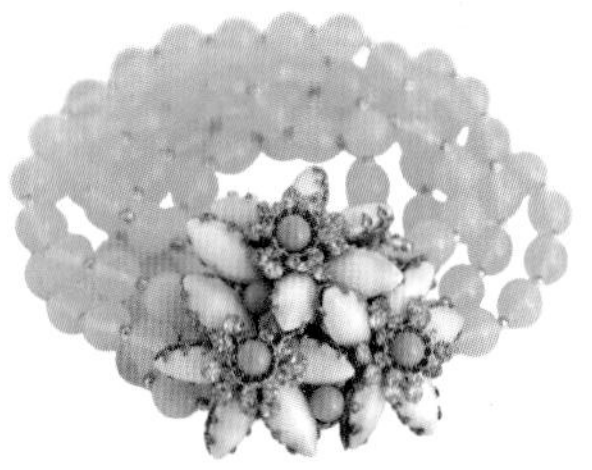

Turquoise glass beaded bracelet, the clasp of which is decorated with three jeweled flowers and functions as a centerpiece. *1960s* ★★☆☆☆

Baby blue and lilac glass flower and crystal basket pin, the flowers and leaves hand-wired onto a gilt brass basket. *1960s* ★★☆☆☆

Gold-plated flower basket brooch with yellow flowers and leaves, emerald rhinestone highlights, and emerald, jade, and peridot green glass flowers. *1960s* ★★☆☆☆

Pin with a cluster of flowerheads in bright shades of pink. *1960s* ★★☆☆☆

Rare large palm tree pin with green and brown beads hand-wired onto a gilt brass backing and embellished with glass bananas, parrots, and butterflies. *1960s* ★★☆☆☆

Gold-plated bangle with flowers made of molded glass and glass beads, and clear crystal rhinestones. *1970s* ★★★★★

Coral clamper bracelet decorated with coral beads and six coral beaded flowers. *1960s* ★★☆☆☆

Five-strand bracelet of peridot glass beads with flower and leaf motifs on a filigree backing, and with emerald rhinestone highlights. *1960s* ★★☆☆☆

Necklace with two strands of emerald glass beads linking seven emerald green flower medallions; with matching earrings. ★★★★☆

Although Hagler's designs were large in scale, he varied the size according to changing fashion.

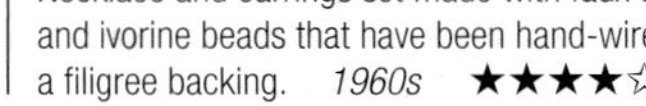

Necklace and earrings set made with faux coral and ivorine beads that have been hand-wired on a filigree backing. *1960s* ★★★★☆

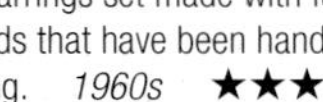

Three-stranded lilac necklace with earrings. The necklace has an extravagant cameo centerpiece surrounded by lilac and seed pearl flowers with five lilac drops. *1960s* ★★★★☆

Necklace and earrings in cornelian (a type of quartz). The necklace is decorated with a floral centerpiece. *1980s* ★★★★☆

"There is certainly no absolute standard of beauty. That precisely is what makes its pursuit so interesting."

JOHN KENNETH GALBRAITH

Blue four-strand necklace with earrings. The necklace clasp is decorated with a three-dimensional floral design, which also functions as a centerpiece. ★★★★☆

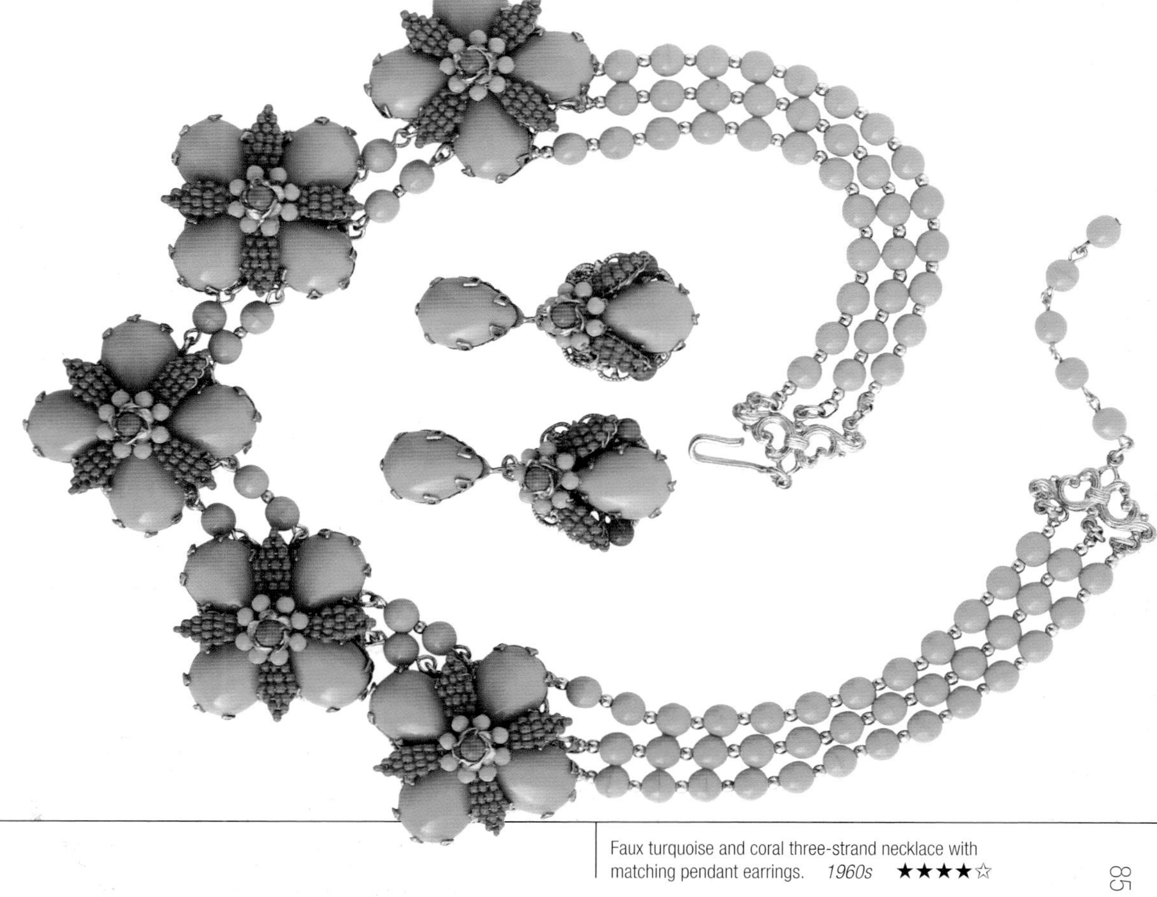

Faux turquoise and coral three-strand necklace with matching pendant earrings. *1960s* ★★★★☆

Two-strand ivorine necklace and matching earrings with ivorine and citrine glass flower centerpiece. *1960s* ★★★★☆

Peach and champagne-colored carved glass flower necklace and earrings. *1960s* ★★★★☆

Earrings decorated with amethyst, peridot, and moonstone glass flowers, rhinestones, and amethyst drops. *1960s* ★★☆☆☆

Prices for Hagler are largely determined by visual impact.

Pair of gilded brass filigree and diamanté drop earrings. *1960s* ★★☆☆☆

Pair of coral and gilded brass three-flower drop earrings. *1960s* ★★☆☆☆

TRIFARI

Worn by high-profile celebrities such as American first lady Mamie Eisenhower in the 1950s and Madonna in the 1990s Hollywood blockbuster *Evita*, Trifari costume jewelry has long held great appeal. The company was established in New York in around 1910 by Italian immigrant Gustavo Trifari and it soon became one of America's pre-eminent costume jewelry-makers. Prestigious publicity and an exclusive clientele were backed by products that featured high-quality designs and materials. From 1930 until 1968, chief designer Alfred Philippe used his talents to produce convincing imitations of precious jewelry using silver, plastic Lucite rhinestones, and faux pearls. Jelly Bellies, 1940s Crown pins, and vintage floral pieces are particularly popular with collectors today.

Patriotic pin and earrings, possibly designed by Alfred Phillippe. *1940s* ★★☆☆☆

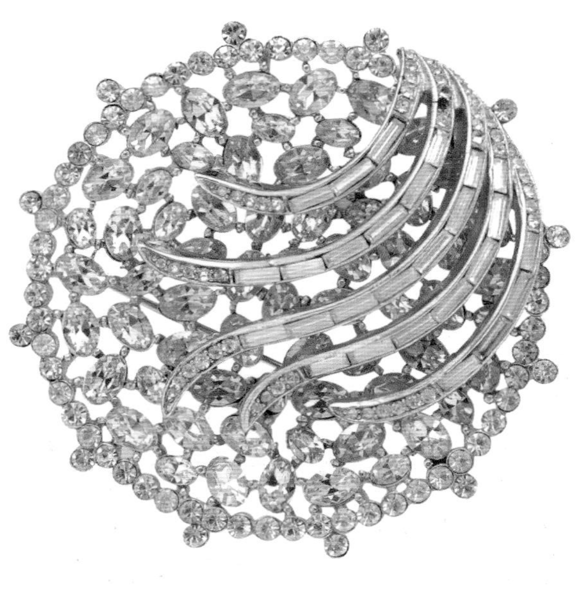

Diamanté and citrine sea motif pin designed by Alfred Philippe. *1940s* ★★★☆☆

Circle pin with invisibly set faux emeralds and a diamanté border. *1950s* ★★☆☆☆

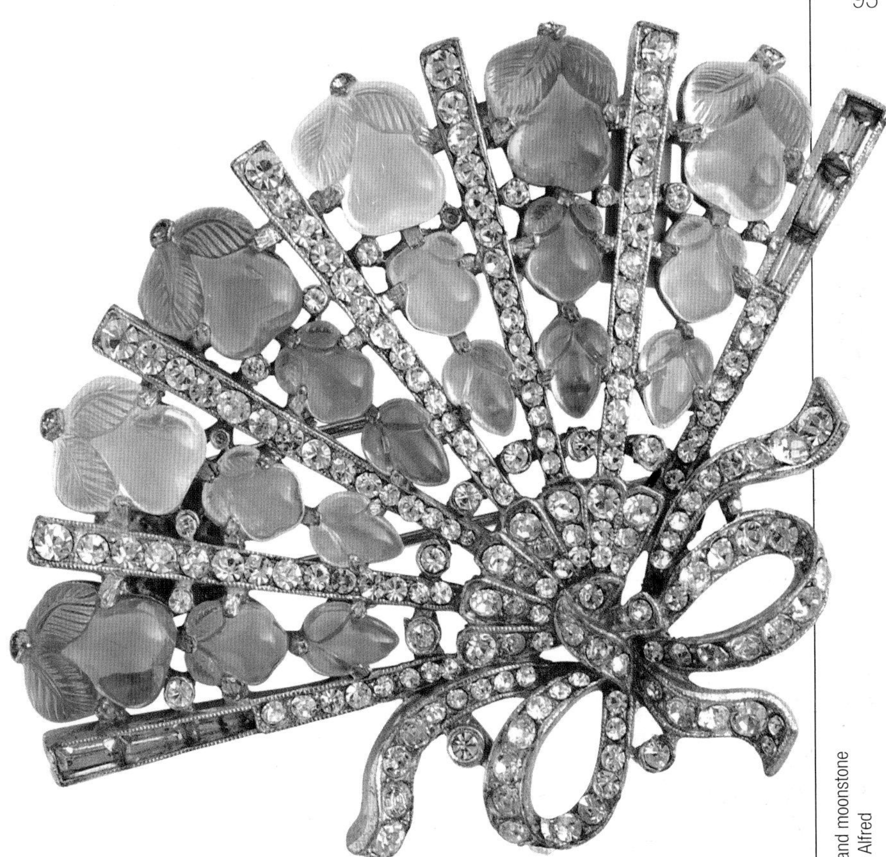

"Don't get mad; get everything!"

Ivana Trump

Fan brooch set with pale blue and moonstone fruit salad stones, designed by Alfred Phillippe. ★★★★★

Hyacinths pin with green, red, blue, and white enameling and pavé-set clear rhinestones. *1940s* ★★★★★

Bouquet of flowers pin, gold-plated with green enameling, milky blue glass stones, and clear rhinestones. *1930s* ★★★★☆

Rose gold-plated fur clip set with faux amethyst stones. ★★★★☆

Very rare floral fur clip of gold and rose-gold vermeil sterling-silver with ruby and clear rhinestones. *1940s* ★★★★☆

Dress and fur clips were very popular during the 1930s and 40s. Pins on the back of pieces were designed to cause as little damage to delicate fabrics as possible.

An essential part of Trifari's success has been the powerful mix of glamorous clientele and prestigious publicity.

Rare, large rhodium-plated sunflower pin with pavé-set and clear citrine rhinestones. *c.1930* ★★★★☆

Brushed gold and diamanté flower pin. *1950s* ★★☆☆☆

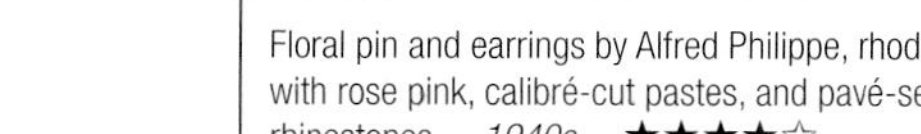

White metal feather pin set with diamanté. *1930s* ★★★☆☆

Floral pin and earrings by Alfred Philippe, rhodium-plated with rose pink, calibré-cut pastes, and pavé-set clear rhinestones. *1940s* ★★★★☆

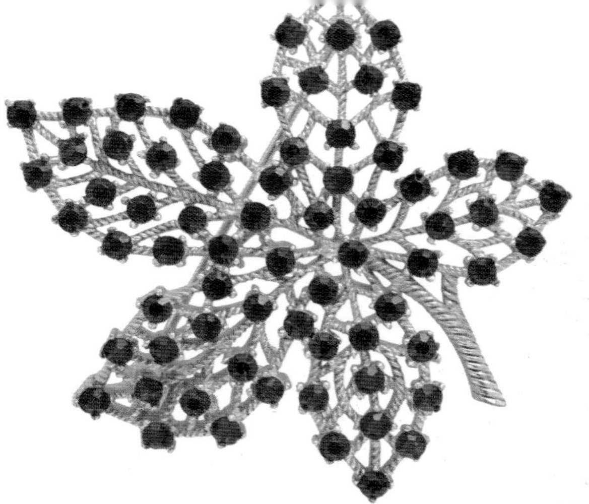

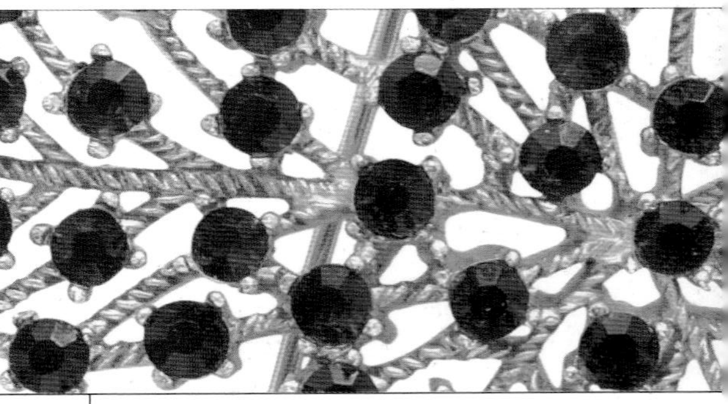

Poured glass camelia pin with gold highlights, inspired by Chanel's camelia pins. *1950s* ★★☆☆☆

Open-backed maple leaf pin set with faux rubies. *1950s* ★☆☆☆☆

Red and green enamel rose pin and earrings set with diamanté highlights. *1950s* ★★☆☆☆

Pair of carnation earrings set with red, green, and clear diamanté. ★★☆☆☆

Trifari made jewelry for first lady Mamie Eisenhower, notably for the 1953 and 1957 inaugural balls.

Pin and earrings with white enamel and turquoise and sapphire cabochons on a yellow metal base. *1950s* ★★☆☆☆

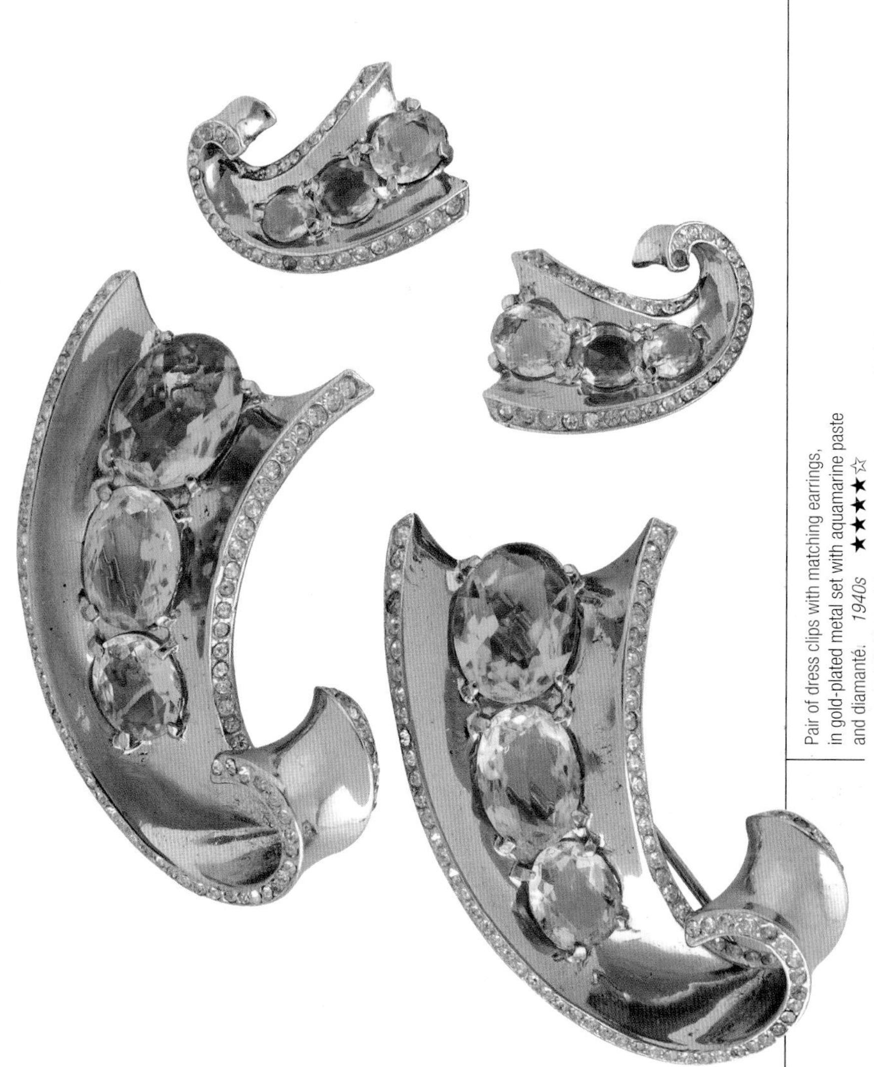

Pair of dress clips with matching earrings, in gold-plated metal set with aquamarine paste and diamanté. *1940s* ★★★★☆

"Jewels of India" pin and earrings of brushed gold finish with emerald green and ruby red cabochons and clear rhinestones. *1950s* ★★★★☆

Miniature flower pin in yellow metal set with pale blue and green enamel and red diamanté. *1950s* ★☆☆☆☆

Pin and earrings with emerald green, ruby red, and sapphire blue rhinestones set around clear rhinestone flowerheads. *1930s* ★★★☆☆

Bow and fruit pin of vermeil sterling silver with large emerald green and small clear rhinestones. *1940s* ★★☆☆☆

Vermeil is gold-plated sterling silver.

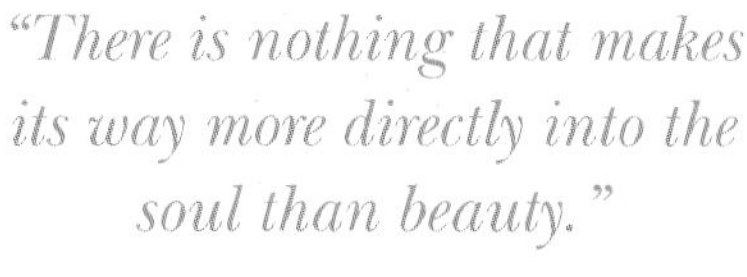

"There is nothing that makes its way more directly into the soul than beauty."

JOSEPH ADDISON

Trifari rhodium-plated necklace with white glass flowerheads and coral cabochon berries. *1930s–40s* ★★★☆☆

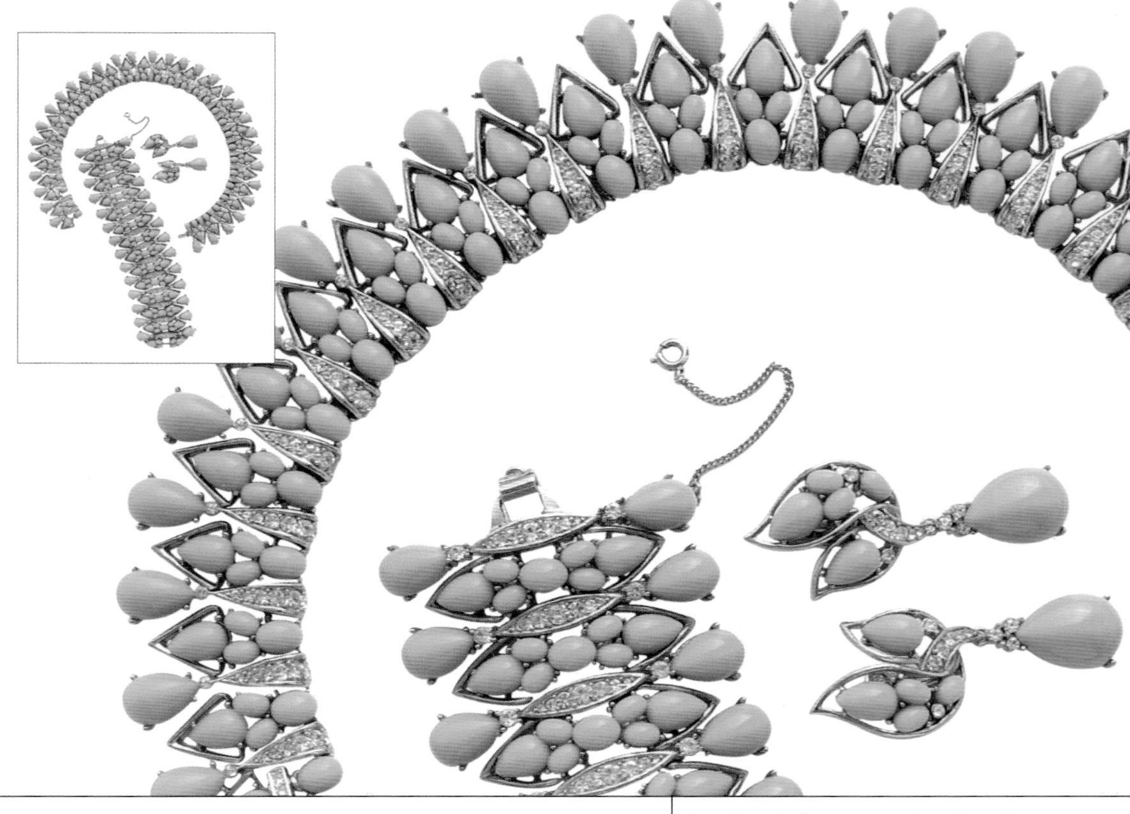

Turquoise cabochon and clear diamanté necklace, bracelet, and earrings. *1950s* ★★★★★

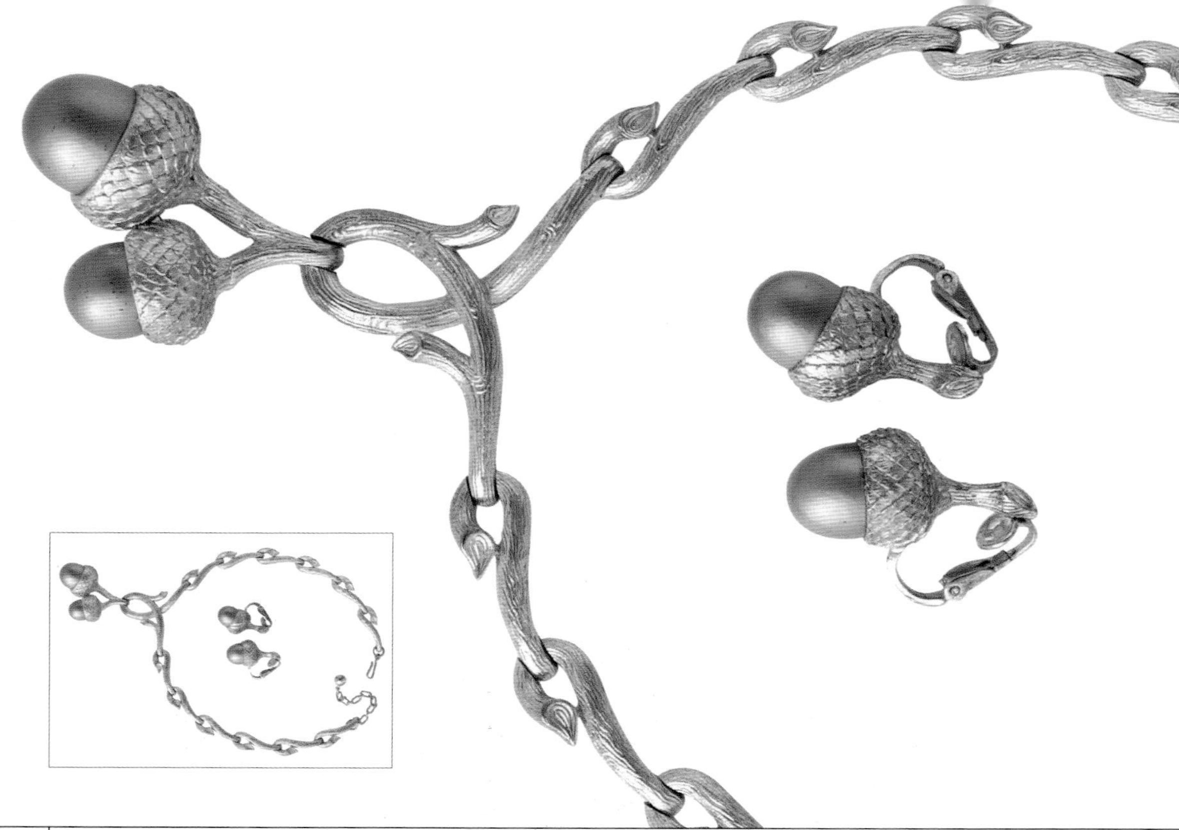

Acorn necklace and earrings in brushed gold metal set with gilded pearls. *1950s* ★★★☆☆

p.331

p.330

p.244

p.328

p.246

p.153

p.27

p.334

p.175

p.202 p.191 p.57

p.197 p.327 p.252

p.331 p.253 p.253

A–Z OF DESIGNERS

During the 20th century, talented and innovative costume jewelers emerged throughout the United States and Europe. Some set up relatively large companies to produce a wide range of styles for all sectors of the market, while others such as Iradj Moini and Sandor Goldberger established small enterprises to design handcrafted limited-edition pieces. Collectively, styles are diverse and range from delicate floral earrings through rhinestone creature pins to heavy abstract necklaces. All makers, from Accessocraft to Zandra Rhodes, have their devotees and the pieces are widely collected today.

Accessocraft eagle astride a globe pin. The eagle is cast of bright gold-tone metal while the globe is made of mottled red Lucite. *1940s* ★☆☆☆☆

Alice Caviness raspberry and leaf pin of textured gold-tone metal with pavé-set faux ruby cabochons. *1960s* ★☆☆☆☆

Alice Caviness umbrella and poodle pin of gilt base metal with prong-set pale and dark amber rhinestones and French jet teardrops. *1970s–80s* ★☆☆☆☆

"Love is the emotion that a woman feels always for a poodle dog and sometimes for a man."

George Jean Nathan

Art apple pin and earrings in colored paste. *1960s* ★★☆☆☆

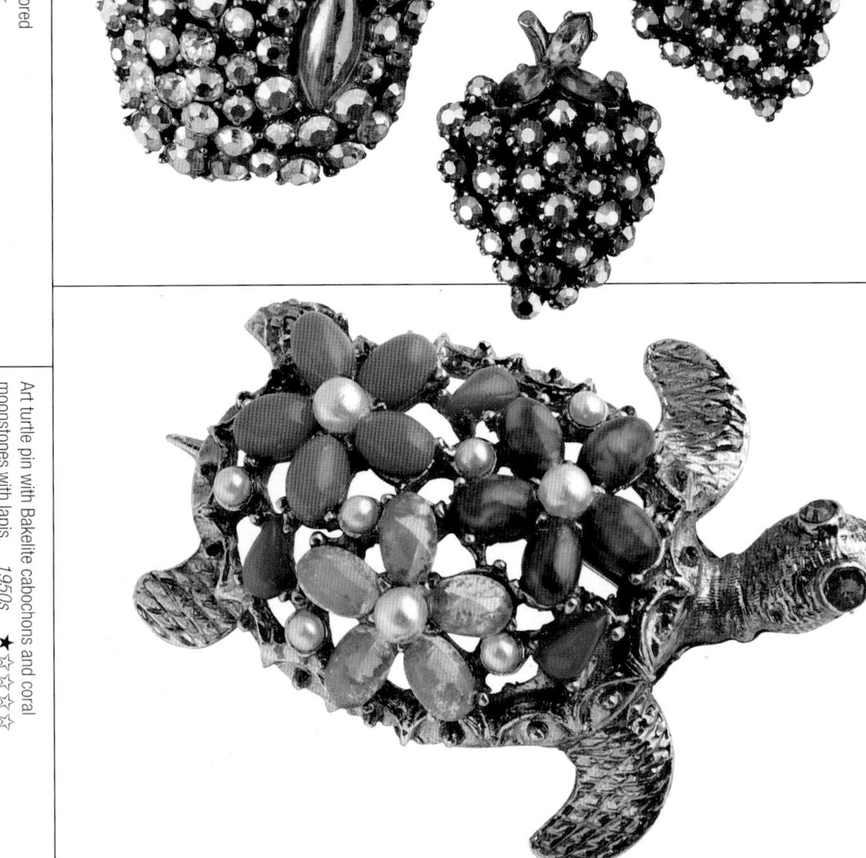

Art turtle pin with Bakelite cabochons and coral moonstones with lapis. *1950s* ★☆☆☆☆

Avon pair of Christmas earrings with faux pearls, ruby rhinestones, and green enameling on gold-washed metal castings. *1980s* ★☆☆☆☆

Avon necklace and earrings from the "Adriatic" collection, designed by José Marie Barrera. ★★☆☆☆

Beaujewels floral pin and earrings with fuchsia pink and pink *aurora borealis* rhinestones set in gold-tone metal. *1940s* ★☆☆☆☆

Balenciaga four-strand couture choker with faceted black glass beads and gilt metal clasp, with turquoise glass cabochons and rhinestones. *c.1960* ★★★★★

"These gems have life in them; their colors speak, say what words fail of."

George Eliot

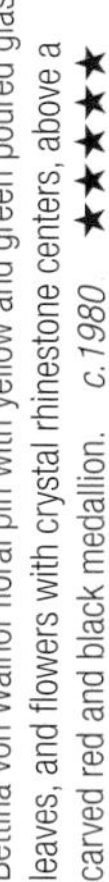

Bettina von Walhof floral pin with yellow and green poured glass leaves, and flowers with crystal rhinestone centers, above a carved red and black medallion. *c.1980* ★★★★★

Marcel Boucher rare poured glass, diamanté, and faux pearl necklace. *1940s* ★★★★★

Marcel Boucher was able to expand his jewelry operation after receiving a lucrative order from Saks Fifth Avenue in 1939.

The dragon has been a symbol of auspicious power in Chinese art and folklore since before the time of written records.

Butler and Wilson gold-plated Oriental dragon pin with blue and green metallic enameling, clear crystal rhinestones, and ruby red cabochon eyes. *Mid-1990s* ★★☆☆☆

Castlecliff gold-plated and enameled Native American chief brooch. *1960s* ★☆☆☆☆

Castlecliff pendant necklace and earrings with gold-plated Mesoamerican heads and motifs, and multicolored semiprecious stone beads. *1940s* ★★★☆☆

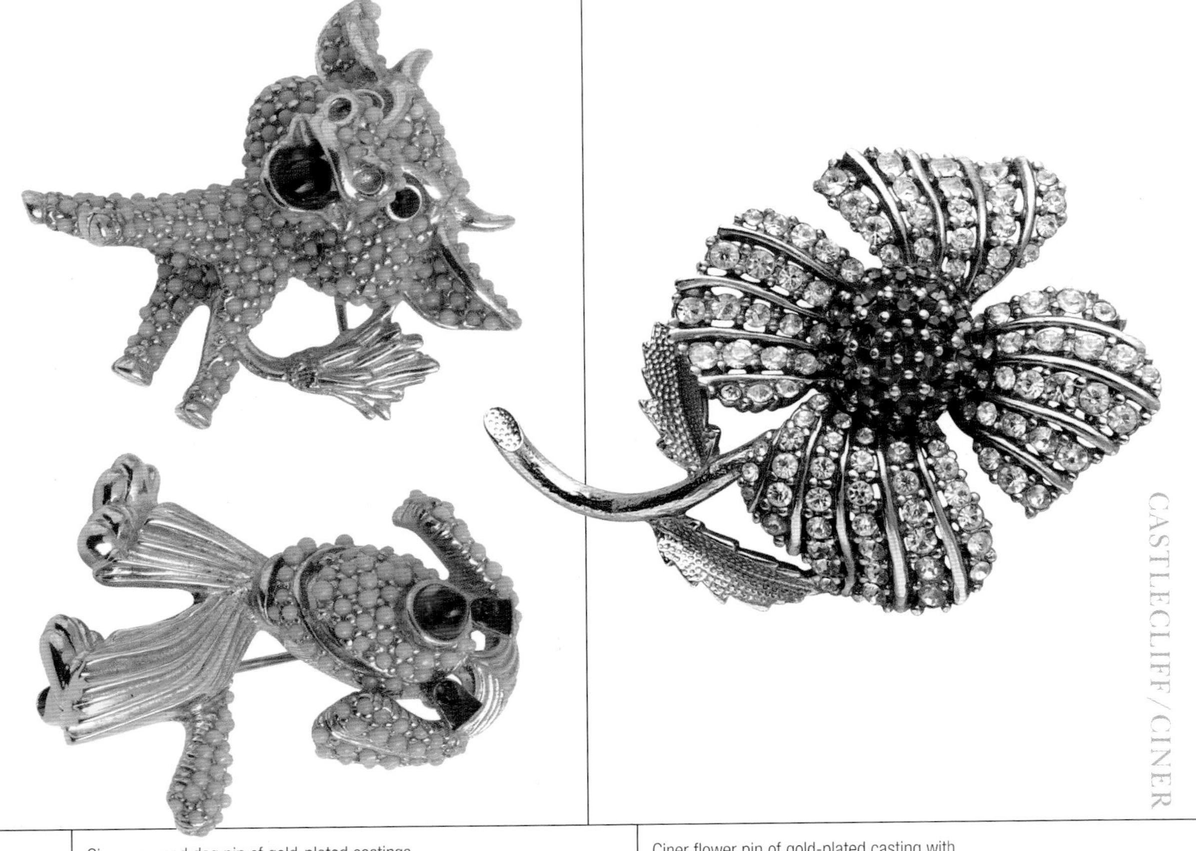

Ciner cow and dog pin of gold-plated castings set with small turquoise and larger ruby glass cabochons. *1950s* ★★★☆☆

Ciner flower pin of gold-plated casting with emerald green and pavé-set clear Swarovski crystal rhinestones. *Mid-1960s* ★★☆☆☆

COPPOLA E TOPPO

Italian brother and sister team Bruno Coppola and Lyda Toppo spent the 1940s working behind the scenes on jewelry for important fashion houses such as Dior and Balenciaga. When the center of the fashion industry switched from Paris to Milan, the Coppola e Toppo company saw its fortunes rise and an increasing number of pieces was produced under its own trademark. The jewelry was extravagant, colorful, and typically worked in beads. Innovative designs, including multistrand necklaces of Murano glass and plastic beads, were successful during the 1960s when fashion-conscious women turned their backs on the diamanté and faux pearl designs of the previous decades.

Coppola e Toppo red glass bead parure consisting of a necklace, bracelet, and earrings with characteristic beaded clasps. *1950s* ★★★★★

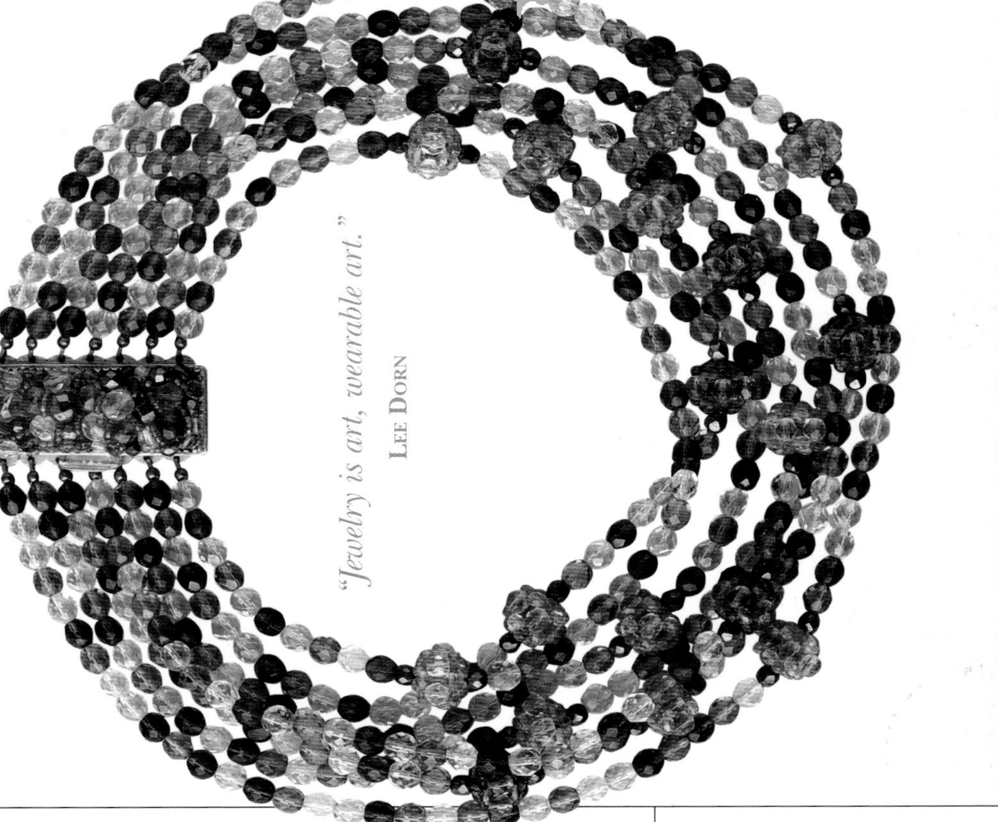

"Jewelry is art, wearable art."

LEE DORN

Coppola e Toppo choker necklace with brown, yellow, amber, and clear Bohemian crystal beads and similarly beaded clasps. *1950s* ★★★★☆

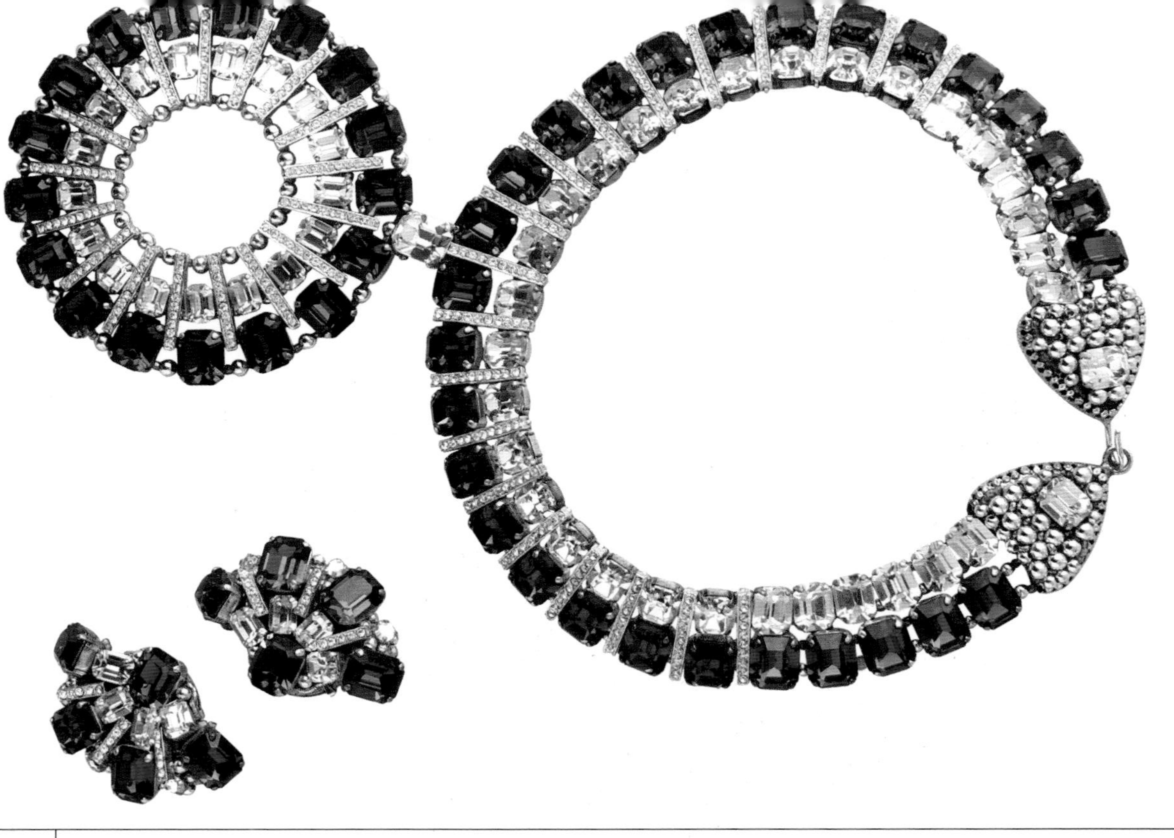

Coppola e Toppo pendant necklace and earrings, designed for Valentino, with faceted sapphire blue and clear Swarovski crystal stones set in gilt metal. *1970* ★★★★★

Cristobal bouquet of flowers pin with multicolored French poured glass and clear rhinestones set in a brass wire frame. *Late 1990s* ★★★★☆

Cristobal butterfly pin with pastel-colored crystal rhinestones and French jet on a rhodium-plated frame. *Late 1990s* ★★☆☆☆

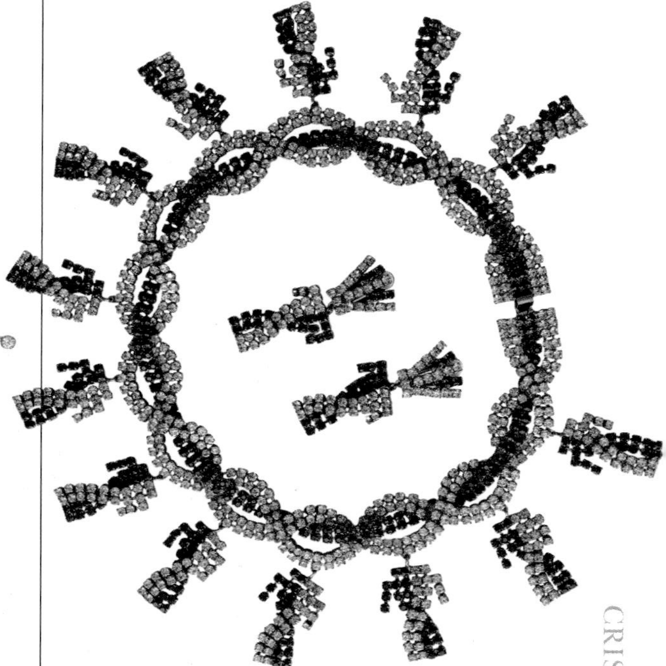

Cristobal necklace with bow pendants and earrings, ruthinium-plated with prong-set amethyst and jet crystal rhinestones. *Late 1990s* ★★☆☆☆

De Nicola floral pin with six gilt metal flowers and faux turquoise cabochon centers encircled by tiny clear rhinestone highlights. *1950s* ★★☆☆☆

"Where flowers bloom so does hope."

FIRST LADY CLAUDIA TAYLOR "LADY BIRD" JOHNSON

De Rosa sterling-silver and gold-plated fur clip with red and clear rhinestones. *1940s* ★★★☆☆

De Rosa sterling-silver brooch with rhinestones and faux sapphires. *1940s* ★★☆☆☆

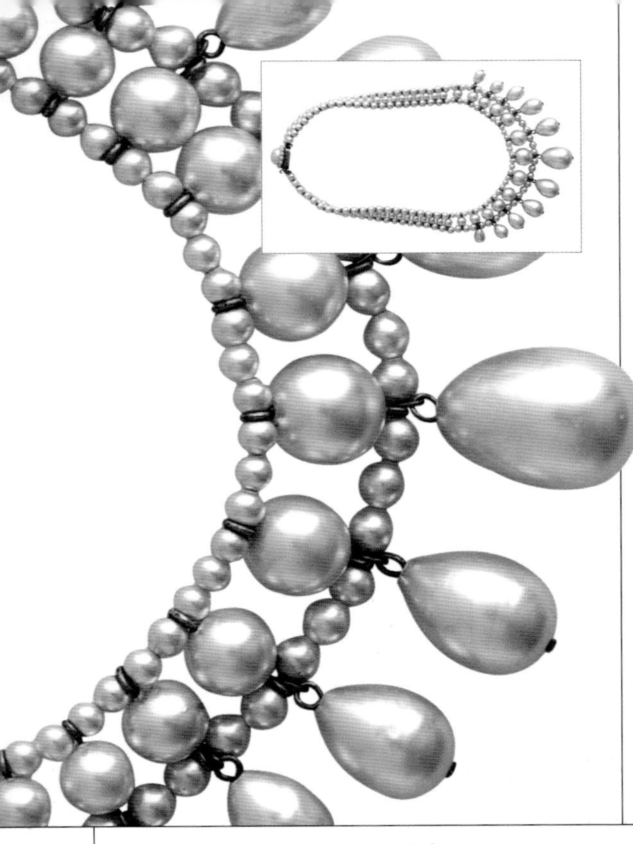

Deposé necklace with strands of faux pearls, faux pearl drops, clear crystal rhinestones, and a silver clasp. *Early 1920s* ★★★☆☆

Deposé pin with faceted glass emerald and clear crystal rhinestones on a silver-plated casting. *1920s* ★★☆☆☆

Eisenberg Ice faceted inset rhinestone bracelet. *1963* ★★☆☆☆

"I love glamorous women. I'm completely behind women dressing up and looking as good as they can."

Elizabeth Hurley

Eisenberg Original bow pin made of base metal set with clear stones. The chunky metal setting and bow design are typical of 1940s' Eisenberg. *1940s* ★★★★☆

EISENBERG

American clothing company Eisenberg Original, established in 1914 by Jonas Eisenberg, initially only produced costume pins to accessorize its own outfits. These pins proved to be so popular with customers that the firm began to sell high-quality jewelry separately, eventually discontinuing its clothing lines in 1958. Designs were typically bold and clean. The use of fine materials such as Swarovski rhinestones make Eisenberg pieces hot collectables today. Particularly popular are early 1940s figural pieces, pins, and necklaces produced during the mid-1940s in sterling silver. Jewelry made from 1930 to 1945 is usually marked "Eisenberg Original", while later pieces are often marked "Eisenberg Ice". The company continues to make costume jewelry today.

Eisenberg Original white metal and diamanté pin the back of one mount is stamped "Sterling". *1940s* ★★★☆☆

Pair of Eisenberg earrings with large stones and set with rhinestones in the frames. ★★★★☆

Pair of Eugene earrings set with turquoise beads and diamanté. *1950s* ★★☆☆☆

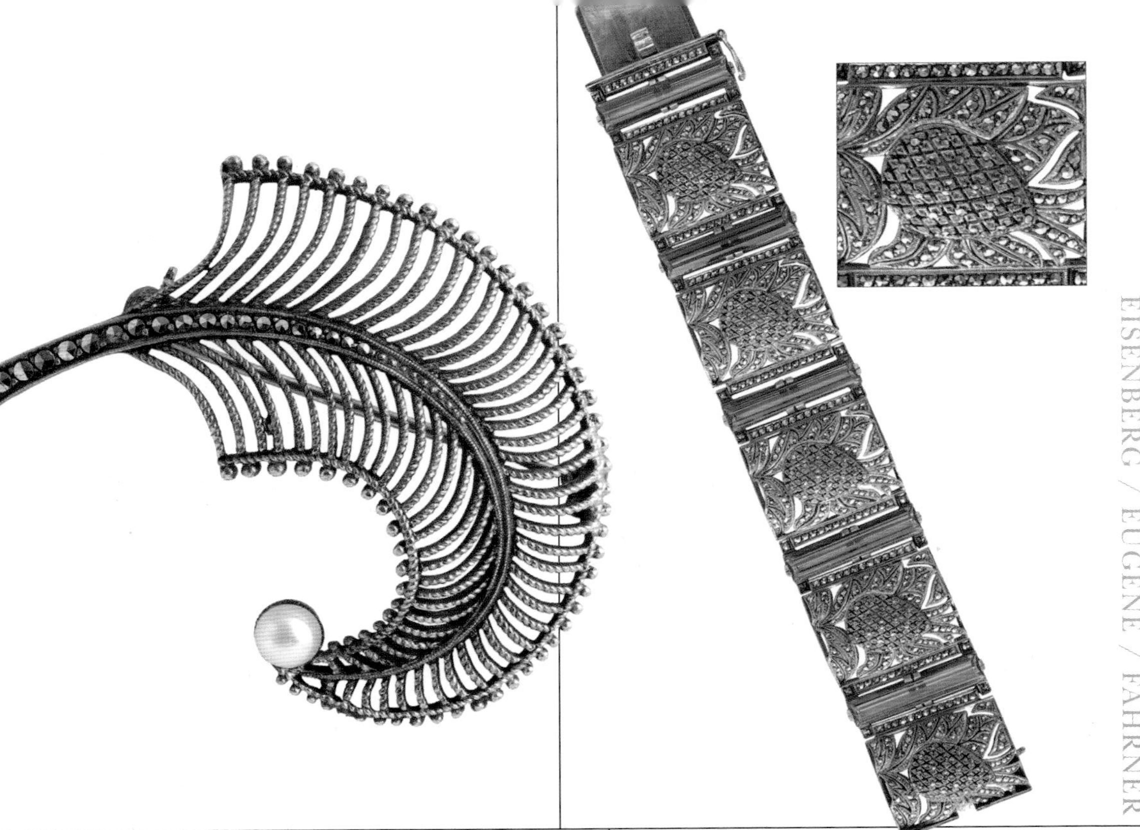

Fahrner stylized leaf pin in silver and marcasite with a single pearl highlight. *1920s* ★★★★☆

Exceptionally rare, museum-quality Fahrner bracelet with marcasite pineapples and aquamarine baguettes. *1930s* ★★★★★

Florenza floral bow pin of antiqued silver tone metal set with rows of small turquoise glass cabochons. *1950s* ★☆☆☆☆

Florenza spring-loaded trembler bird pin with two colors of green faceted rhinestones and a central inset faux pearl. *1950s* ★☆☆☆☆

Fred A. Block cat pin made of vermeil sterling silver with turquoise glass beads on the whiskers and tail, and clear crystal rhinestone eyes. *1940s* ★★★☆☆

"Two things are aesthetically perfect in the world – the clock and the cat."

EMILE AUGUSTE CHARTIER

p.59

p.51

p.339

p.338

p.37

p.118

p.271

p.155

p.275

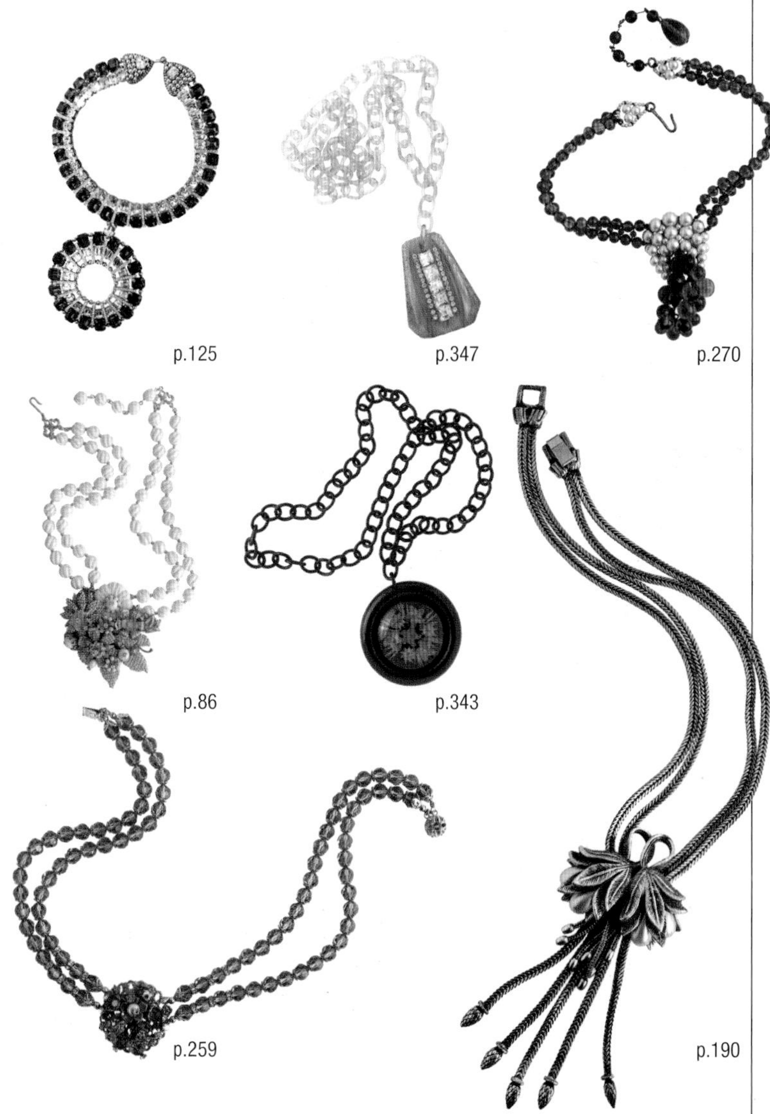

p.125

p.347

p.270

p.86

p.343

p.259

p.190

"I take a pinch of Byzantine, a hint of Etruscan, a sprinkling of Celtic or Egyptian. And I make a Goossens cocktail."

ROBERT GOOSSENS

Goossens-style necklace with gilded stampings and glass coral cabouchons, crystals, and faux pearl drops. *1940s* ★★★★☆

Gripoix glass bracelet; the clasp is marked "Made in France". *1930s* ★★★☆☆

Maison Gripoix flower pin with poured glass leaves and turquoise, emerald, and black glass cabochons in an antiqued gilt metal frame. *1940s* ★★★★★

Har dragon necklace and earrings in enameled yellow metal set with *aurora borealis* stones. *c.1955* ★★★★★

Made in New York in the 1950s, Har jewelry has a limited but distinctive range of fantastical designs.

Har pair of cobra head earrings with *aurora borealis* lava stones, green enamel, and topaz crystal rhinestones on gold-plated castings. *1950s* ★★★☆☆

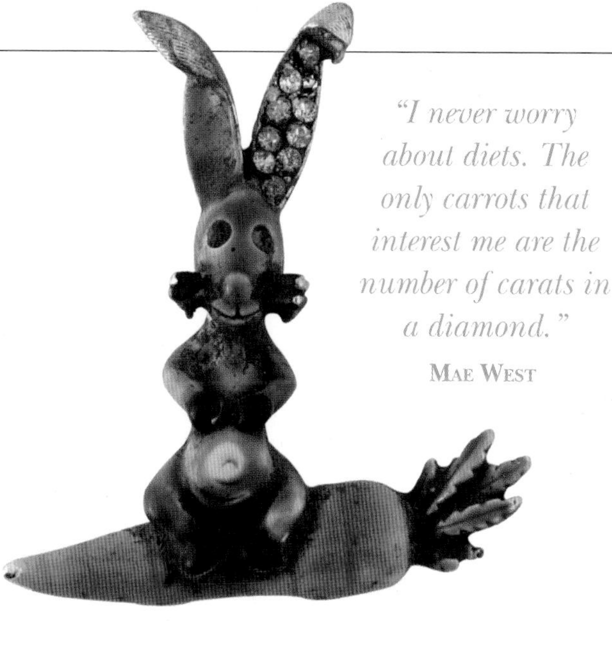

"I never worry about diets. The only carrots that interest me are the number of carats in a diamond."

Mae West

Har rabbit on a carrot pin cast in gold-tone metal with green and red enameling and crystal rhinestones. *1950s* ★☆☆☆☆

Hattie Carnegie pin with multiple scrolls highlighted with colored enamels and pearlescent drops. *1950s* ★★☆☆☆

"A strong piece of jewelry can make a simple outfit look elegant."

Georgio Armani

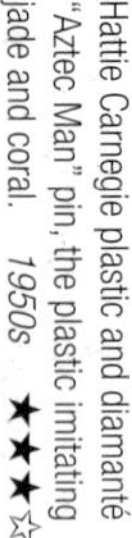

Hattie Carnegie plastic and diamanté "Aztec Man" pin, the plastic imitating jade and coral. *1950s* ★★★☆☆

Histoire de Verre flower pin with gold-plated brass stem and stamens, and with sapphire blue and emerald poured glass petals and leaves and rhinestone stigmas. *1990s* ★★★☆☆

Histoire de Verre floral motifs necklace and earrings with amethyst and jonquil poured glass petals and amethyst glass bead centers. *1990s* ★★★★★

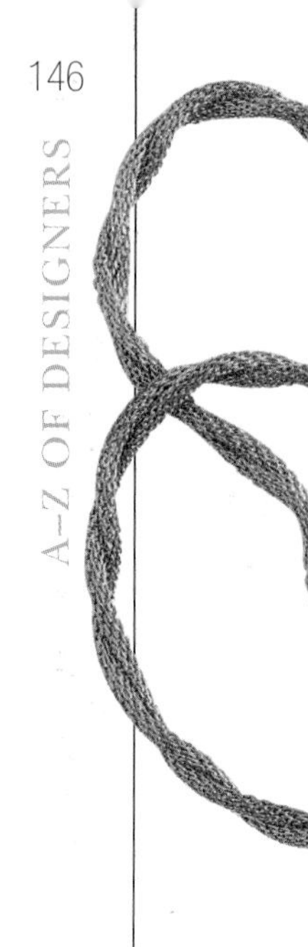

Hobé necklace and earrings of flower form, with iridescent glass petals and inset diamanté and detachable pendant. *1960s* ★★☆☆☆

"There are always flowers for those who want to see them."

HENRI MATISSE

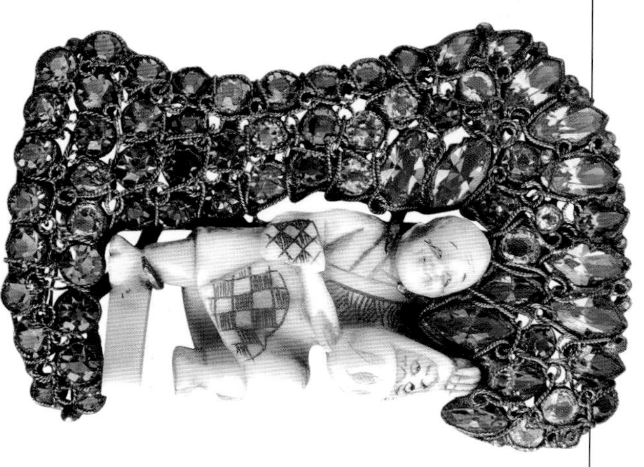

Hobé pin with brightly colored clustered stones supporting an Oriental figure. ★★★★★

Gigantic Hobé rose-gold sterling pin with an ornate floral and scrolled design. *1940s* ★★★★★

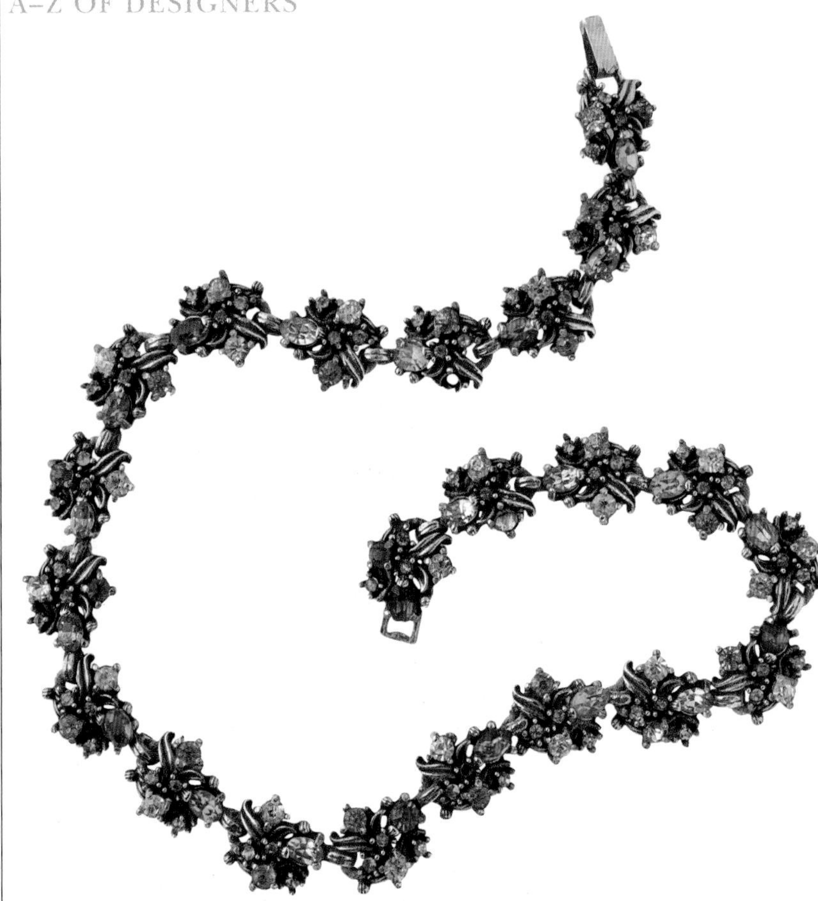

Hollycraft necklace with gilt metal castings set with turquoise, aquamarine, pink, orange, and clear rhinestones of diverse cuts. *1950s* ★★☆☆☆

"Of two evils, choose the prettier."

CAROLYN WELLS

"The earth laughs in flowers."

E. E. Cummings

Ian St Gielar flower pin with iridescent shell petals and an amber red glass center encircled by topaz crystal rhinestones. *Late 1990s* ★★★☆☆

Iradj Moini bouquet of flowers pin and earrings with ruby red, olivine, and amber hand-blown French glass petals, carved jade leaves, and clear rhinestone highlights. *Early 1990s* ★★★★☆

Iradj Moini *en tremblant* rose motif pin with prong-set, round-cut clear rhinestones on a ruthinium-plated frame. *Mid-1990s* ★★★★★

Iranian-born Iradj Moini began designing catwalk jewelry for Oscar de la Renta, fashion designer, in the late 1980s. Pieces are typically large and exquisitely detailed.

Jomaz pin with a gold-colored jester's head in a blue hat and green collar with bells. ★★☆☆☆

Jomaz "Chinaman" green glass, enamel, and diamanté pin. *1960s–70s* ★☆☆☆☆

Jomaz pair of earrings in white metal set with baguette and round paste stones and faux pearls. *1940s* ★★☆☆☆

"Life exists for the love of music or beautiful things."

G. K. Chesterton

Kenneth Jay Lane bracelet set with multicolored stones on a gold-colored background, with matching earrings. ★★★★☆

Kenneth Jay Lane pair of Indian-inspired earrings, with ruby and amethyst glass stones surrounded by clear diamantés. *1960s* ★★★☆☆

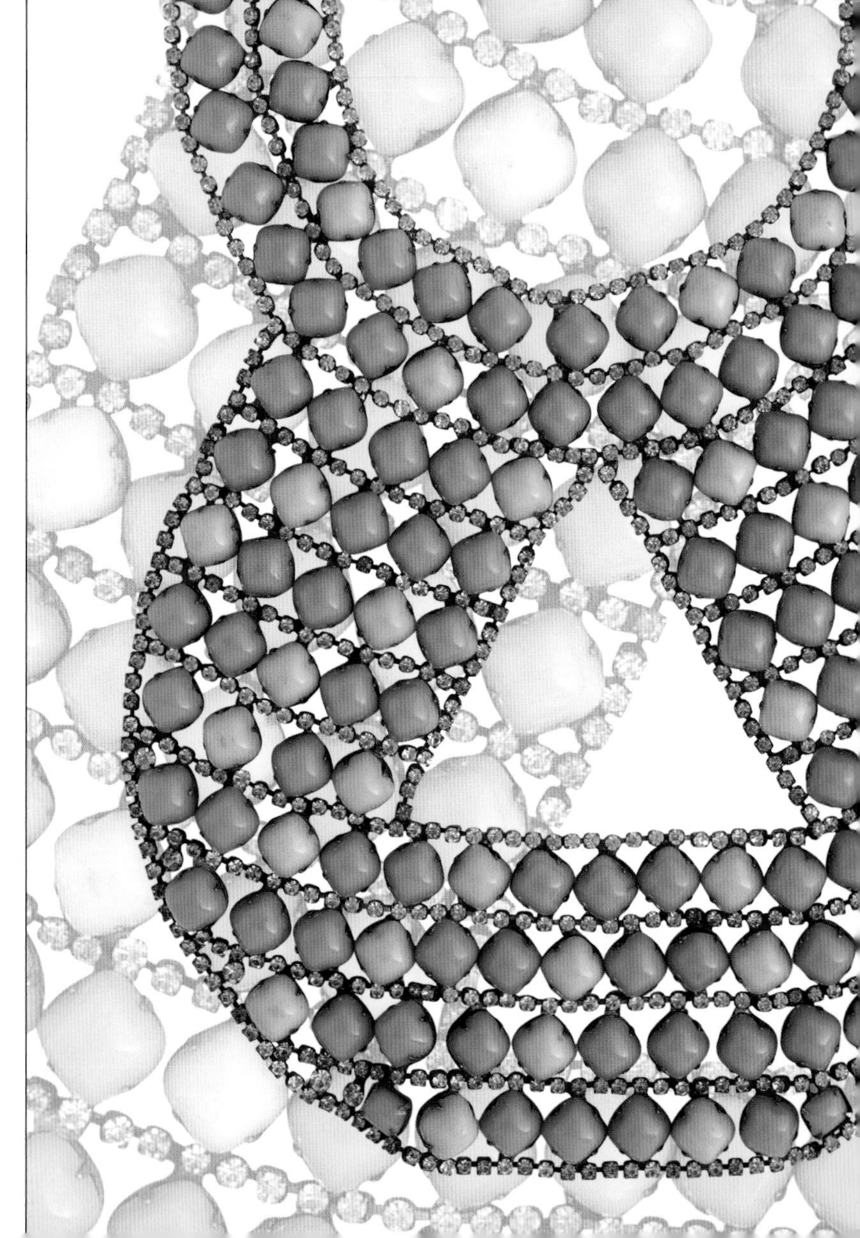

KENNETH JAY LANE

Beginning his career in the art department at *Vogue* magazine, Kenneth Jay Lane (b.1930) was championed by the legendary editor Diana Vreeland. In 1963, after creating shoes for Dior and earrings for Arnold Scaasi, he founded a successful costume jewelry company. Despite affordable prices and high volume sales through shopping channels in recent years, his client list has featured celebrities such as Elizabeth Taylor, Jackie Kennedy Onassis, and Diana, Princess of Wales. His pieces often incorporate styles of historical periods from Ancient Egyptian through Medieval to Art Deco and, during the 1960s–70s, many pieces were adorned with Asian motifs. Highly collectible designs dating from before the late 1970s are marked "K.J.L.", while his later jewelry is signed "Kenneth Lane" or "Kenneth Jay Lane".

Kenneth Jay Lane turquoise blue glass and clear rhinestone bib necklace. This is typical of Lane's extravagant 1960s designs. ★★★★

Kramer choker necklace with turquoise glass crosses on gold-tone metal castings. *1950s* ★☆☆☆☆

Kramer leopard pin of gilt metal with black enamel spots, emerald rhinestone eyes, and a saddle of pavé-set clear rhinestones. *1950s* ★☆☆☆☆

"Wearing costume jewelry is like wearing glass slippers. You can feel like you're going to the ball, even if you're not."

KENNETH JAY LANE

Larry Vrba amethyst flower pin with jeweled petals and pale pink leaves. *1980s* ★★★☆☆

Larry Vrba cerise and clear diamanté flower pin set with keystone petals. *1980s* ★★★☆☆

Larry Vrba shell pin decorated with a diamanté and faux turquoise flower and faux coral. ★★★☆☆

Discoveries of Stone Age jewelry suggest that sea shells have been used for adornment for thousands of years.

L'Atelier de Verre pair of floral earrings of green poured glass and clear crystal rhinestones in gold-plated settings. *c.2000* ★★★☆☆

L'Atelier de Verre bracelet with four strands of dark amethyst poured glass beads and a pansy clasp with black, amethyst, and green poured glass. *c.2000* ★★☆☆☆

LEA STEIN

Instantly recognizable, Lea Stein's unique rhodoid (multiple, bake-bonded sheets of cellulose acetate) jewelry has become highly collectible. Parisian-born Stein (b.1931) turned her creative talents to the production of costume jewelry in 1969. Using laminated layers of brightly colored rhodoid cut into geometrical shapes and layered with other materials such as lace or metal, Stein created a wide variety of striking pins and other jewelry. Imagery included animals, portraits, hearts, and celebrity figures such as Joan Crawford and Elvis Presley. One of her most sought-after pieces is the "Ballerina" pin, inspired by the character Scarlett O'Hara in *Gone with the Wind.* Stein ceased production in 1981, but after increased demand from the United States, she returned to designing new pins in 1988 and continues to make her unusual jewelry today.

Lea Stein "Corolle" pin made of laminated rhodoid. *Early 1980s* ★★☆☆☆

Lea Stein Edelweiss flower pin made of red, pink, orange, brown, green, and white laminated rhodoid. *Late 1980s* ★★☆☆☆

> *"Every once in a while a girl has to indulge herself."*
> **SARAH JESSICA PARKER AS CARRIE BRADSHAW**

Lea Stein owl pin made from laminated rhodoid. *Late 1980s* ★★☆☆☆

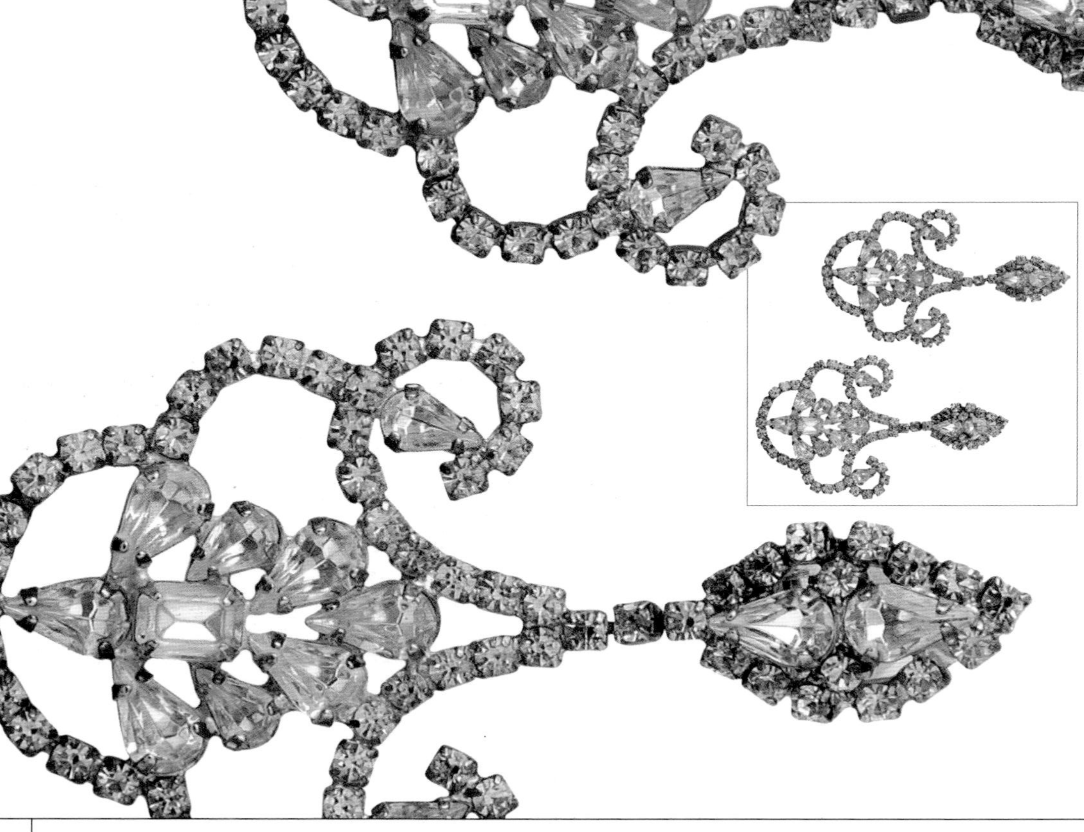

Les Bernard pair of interlaced scroll-form pendant earrings made of marcasite, with clear pale green rectangular and pear-cut rhinestones. *1980s* ★★☆☆☆

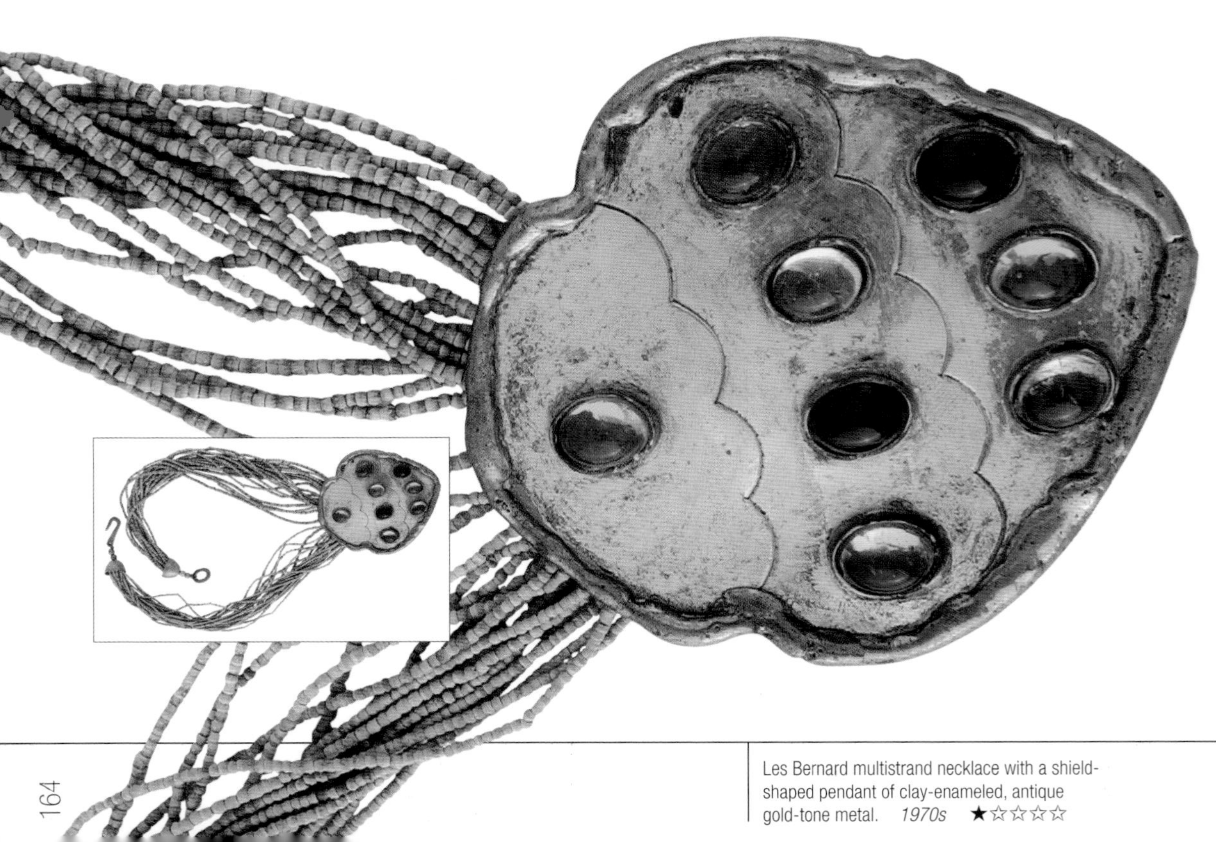

Les Bernard multistrand necklace with a shield-shaped pendant of clay-enameled, antique gold-tone metal. *1970s* ★☆☆☆☆

Extremely rare Lily Daché pin in the form of a single flower encrusted with clear and green stones. *1940s* ★★★★☆

Lisner exotic flower pin in brushed gold-tone metal with faux pearls. *1950s* ★☆☆☆☆

"To create a little flower is the labour of ages."

William Blake

Lisner Maltese cross-shaped pin inlaid with faceted diamanté. *1960s* ★☆☆☆☆

"Nothing happened in the sixties except that we all dressed up."

John Lennon

Marvella triple chain necklace of gold-tone metal with faux pearls and three cartouches with large, navette-cut clear rhinestones. *1970s* ★☆☆☆☆

BOLD BLOOMS

p.99
p.121
p.157
p.145
p.98
p.157
p.195
p.128
p.162

p.149 p.237 p.141
p.315 p.218 p.97
p.96 p.96 p.13

Marvella pin and pair of earrings with yellow faceted rhinestones and scroll forms. *1960s* ★★☆☆☆

Matisse maple leaf pin with red enamel on copper and copper berry highlights. *Mid-1950s* ★★☆☆☆

Mazer Bros. pair of gold-plated earrings, with large pale blue octagon crystal stones, small clear crystal rhinestones, and faux pearls. *1950s* ★★☆☆☆

Mazer Bros. ruby glass and diamanté inset necklace and earrings. *1930s* ★★★★★

Monet cross pin of gold-plated casting set with pear-shaped faux pearls and navette-, baguette-, and round-cut rhinestones. *1980s* ★★☆☆☆

"A thing of beauty is a joy forever: its loveliness increases; it will never pass into nothingness."

John Keats

Napier silver-tone metal and green Bakelite necklace and earrings. *1940s* ★★★★☆

Napier bowling theme bracelet in yellow-tone metal decorated with plastic bowling pins and balls. *1950s* ★★☆☆☆

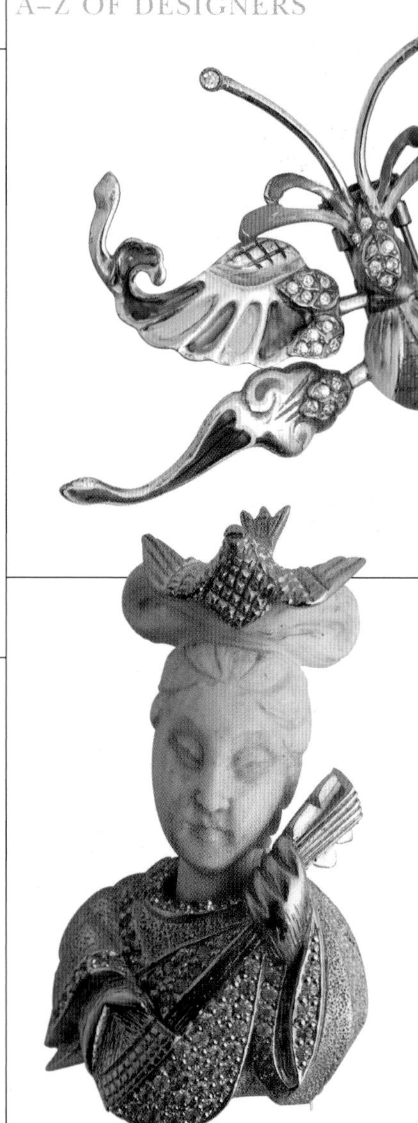

Nettie Rosenstein butterfly fur clip in sterling silver, gold-plate, and enamel. Rosenstein's pieces are very rare. *1940s* ★★★★☆

Nettie Rosenstein figural diamanté and faux ivory brooch. *1940s* ★★★☆☆

"Everything has its beauty but not everyone sees it."

CHINESE PROVERB

Panetta floral motif pin of antiqued gilt metal, the center and petals with pavé-set clear crystal rhinestones. *1950s* ★★☆☆☆

Panetta ring of platinum colored metal set with bands and navette-shaped cups of pale amethyst crystal rhinestones. *1960s* ★☆☆☆☆

PENNINO

Intricate workmanship characterizes the work of the New York jewelry and watch case firm founded by brothers Frank and Oreste Pennino in the mid-1920s. Pieces were largely made by skilled Italian *émigrés* such as Adrian Scannavino and Beneditto Panetta, and used fine materials such as the best-quality Austrian rhinestones. Unlike pieces by many rival firms, designs often featured generously thick sections of sterling silver or 14-carat gold-plate, and settings for stones were cast in silver. Favorite forms included bows, flowers, and scrolls. Abstract designs and sweeping curves were typical, and pieces were often marked "Pennino" in script. Manufacture of Pennino costume jewelry continued until 1961.

Pennino pin in the form of allium flowers; with blue glass and diamanté, stamped "Pennino Sterling". *1940s* ★★☆☆☆

Pennino pin with blue glass petals, diamanté highlights, and red glass centers; marked "Pennino Sterling". *1940s* ★★☆☆☆

"As the sun colors flowers, so does art color life."

JOHN LUBBOCK

Pennino plated, faceted green, and clear diamanté pin with scrolling forms. *1940s* ★☆☆☆☆

Rebajes copper pin with three leaves; the back is stamped with the Rebajes name. *1940s* ★☆☆☆☆

Rebajes stylized "African head" copper pin, with copper wire necklace and earrings. *Late 1940s* ★★★☆☆

Regency gold-plated necklace and earrings, with prong-set *aurora borealis* and emerald green round and teardrop cabochons. *1950s* ★★★☆☆

Regency gold-plated flower and leaf pin made in Canada, with lime green navettes and carved powder blue glass stones. *Late 1950s–70s* ★★☆☆☆

Réja flower pin of vermeil sterling silver with green, pink, and white enameling, carved aquamarine pastes, and clear rhinestones. *c.1939* ★★★★☆

Réja bracelet, pin, and earrings of vermeil sterling silver with opaque pinkish-red cabochons and clear rhinestones. *1947* ★★★★☆

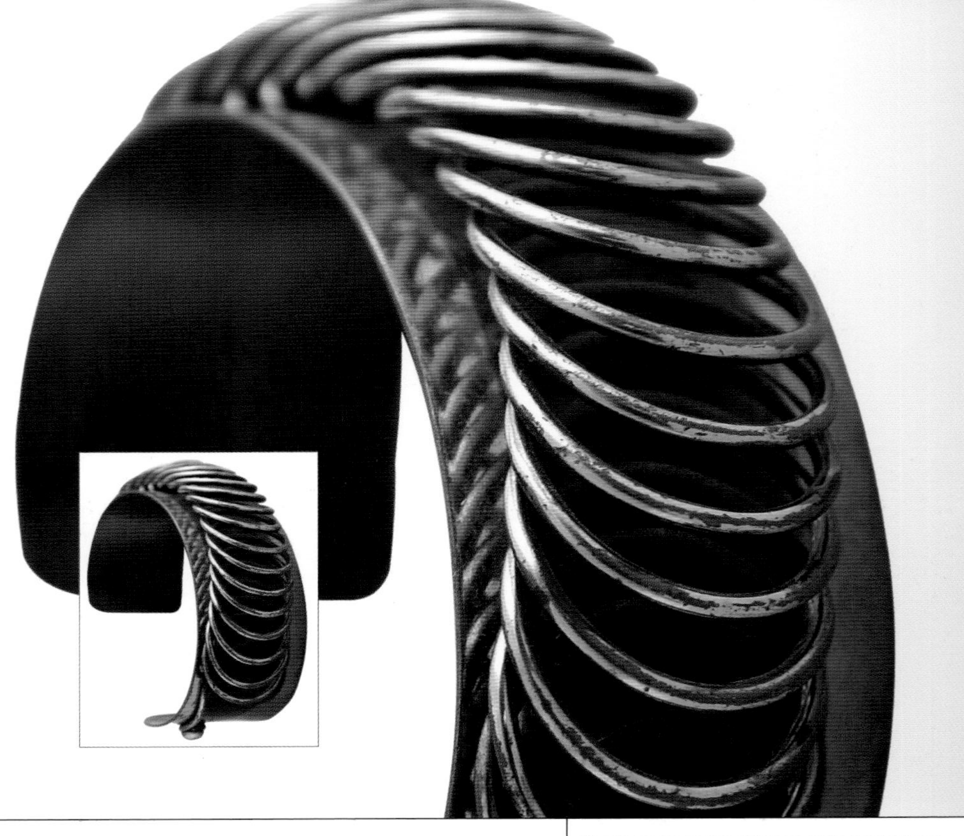

Renoir copper bangle with rope-molded edges and hooped wire decoration. *Mid-1950s* ★★☆☆☆

Robert de Mario pin and earrings with pale blue crystal cabochons and rhinestones set in silver gilt metal. *Late 1950s* ★★☆☆☆

Robert de Mario floral motif pin of gilt metal with large faceted emerald green crystal stones and small clear crystal rhinestone highlights. *1950s* ★★☆☆☆

Robert pair of brass and faceted diamanté earrings. ★★☆☆☆

Robert pin set with a circle of stones and scroll details around a faceted crescent. *1930s* ★★★★☆

Sandor pin and clip earrings with pink molded glass berries and green enamel leaves. *1950s* ★★☆☆☆

Sandor pin with three yellow flowers sprouting from a triangular green pot. *1930s* ★★★★☆

SCHREINER

The exclusive costume jewelry of Bavarian-born maker Henry Schreiner continues to attract collectors' attention and high prices today. After working as a blacksmith, Schreiner left his homeland for the United States, where he started work at a buckle company. A talented designer, Schreiner set up his own costume jewelry company in New York during the 1940s. His exuberant pieces, characterized by unconventional combinations of colors, paste stones, and inverted-set rhinestones, made him popular with stars such as Marilyn Monroe. High-quality diamanté and crystal were also widely used, and pieces were hand-set to high standards. He went on to design jewelry and other small accessories for fashion houses such as Dior. Schreiner jewelry, particularly the full parures (sets), are harder to find than pieces by other costume jewelry-makers of the period.

Schreiner pin with tightly clustered, long green glass stones radiating from a central stone. *1940s* ★★☆☆☆

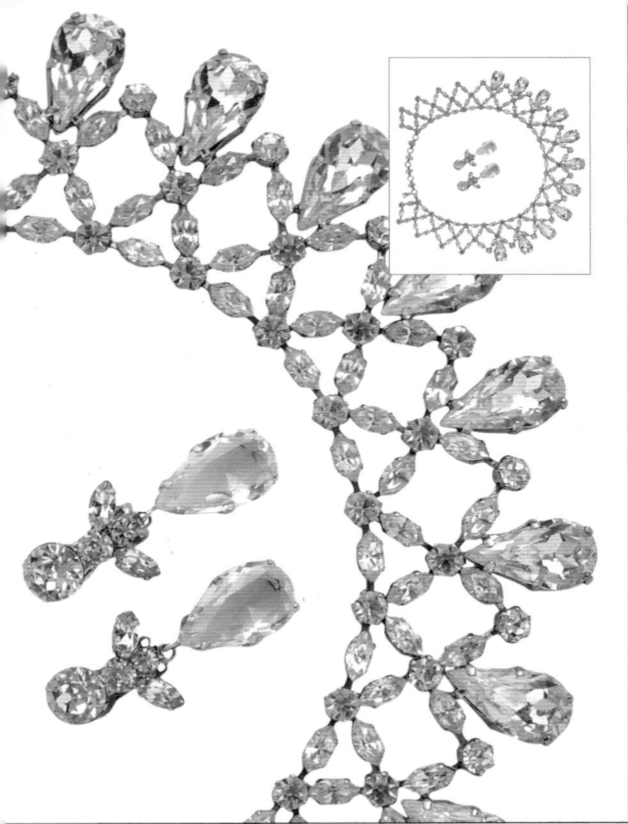

Schreiner necklace and earrings set with faceted clear paste stones. *1950s* ★★★★★

Selro metal bracelet with glass beads in shades of blue, with matching earrings. *1950s* ★★☆☆☆

Selro is renowned for the use of faces in its designs.

Selro Oriental heads pendant necklace and earrings, in red Lucite with a silver-plated chain. *Late 1950s* ★★☆☆☆

Tortolani "Bolo" style necklace in silver-plated pewter wth faux pearl highlights. *Early 1970s* ★★☆☆☆

Pewter is an alloy made up of tin, copper, and sometimes various other metals. Used by the Ancient Egyptians, it became increasingly popular during the 13th century.

Tortolani devil pin, hand-cast in antiqued gold-plated pewter with ruby red crystal rhinestone eyes. *c.1960* ★★☆☆☆

Vendome clamper bracelet in yellow metal set with faux citrine and topaz cabochons. *1950s* 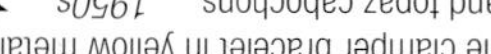

Vendome feather pin in white metal set with simulated pearls and diamanté. *1950s* ★★☆☆☆

Vendome yellow pompom flower pin and earrings, with plastic petals and *aurora borealis* highlights, and yellow metal stem and leaves. *1950s* ★★☆☆☆

"I'm trying to do the same thing but in a different way."

VIVIENNE WESTWOOD

Vivienne Westwood faux pearl choker with a royal orb and cross finial studded with pavé-set clear crystal rhinestones. *1980s* ★★☆☆☆

Vogue gold-plated white metal lily corsage pin set with glass and diamanté; marked "Sterling". *1930s* ★★★☆☆

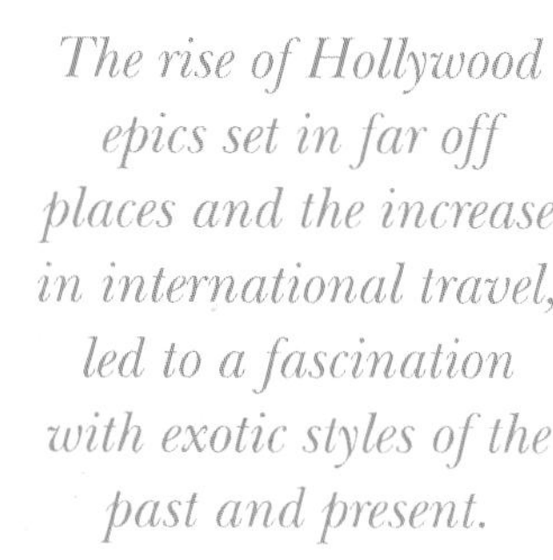

Vogue sterling-silver, gold-plated blackamoor brooch and earrings. *1940s* ★★★☆☆

The rise of Hollywood epics set in far off places and the increase in international travel, led to a fascination with exotic styles of the past and present.

Warner mechanical day and night flower pin, in which the petals open and close. *1940s* ★★☆☆☆

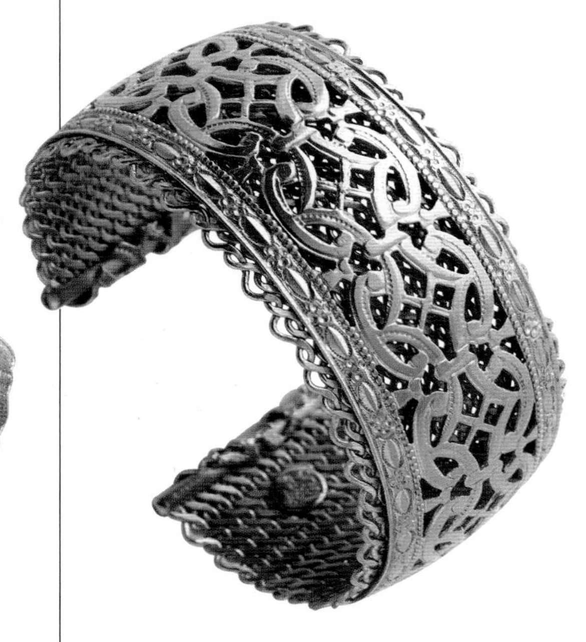

Volupté open bangle of gold-tone metal, the inner band of wire mesh, the outer band pierced and chased with arabesque patterns. *Pre-1960s* ★☆☆☆☆

WEISS

Known for its use of exceptional Austrian crystal rhinestones, the Weiss company is enjoying renewed interest from collectors. After honing his jewelry skills at Coro, Albert Weiss established his own small costume jewelry firm in New York in 1942. By the 1950s, sheer demand for Weiss pieces meant some of the output had to be contracted out to Hollycraft. The majority of Weiss designs are floral or figural, but Art Deco-style ranges were also produced. Standards of craftsmanship were high, materials were of high quality, and rhinestones exhibited an exceptional purity of color. Pieces using reproductions of fine German smoky crystal, known as "black diamonds" and 1950s designs featuring iridescent Swarovski *aurora borealis* rhinestones were particularly innovative and remain popular today.

Weiss pair of earrings with central pink rough-cut stone surrounded by lilac, green, and pink baguettes. ★★☆☆☆

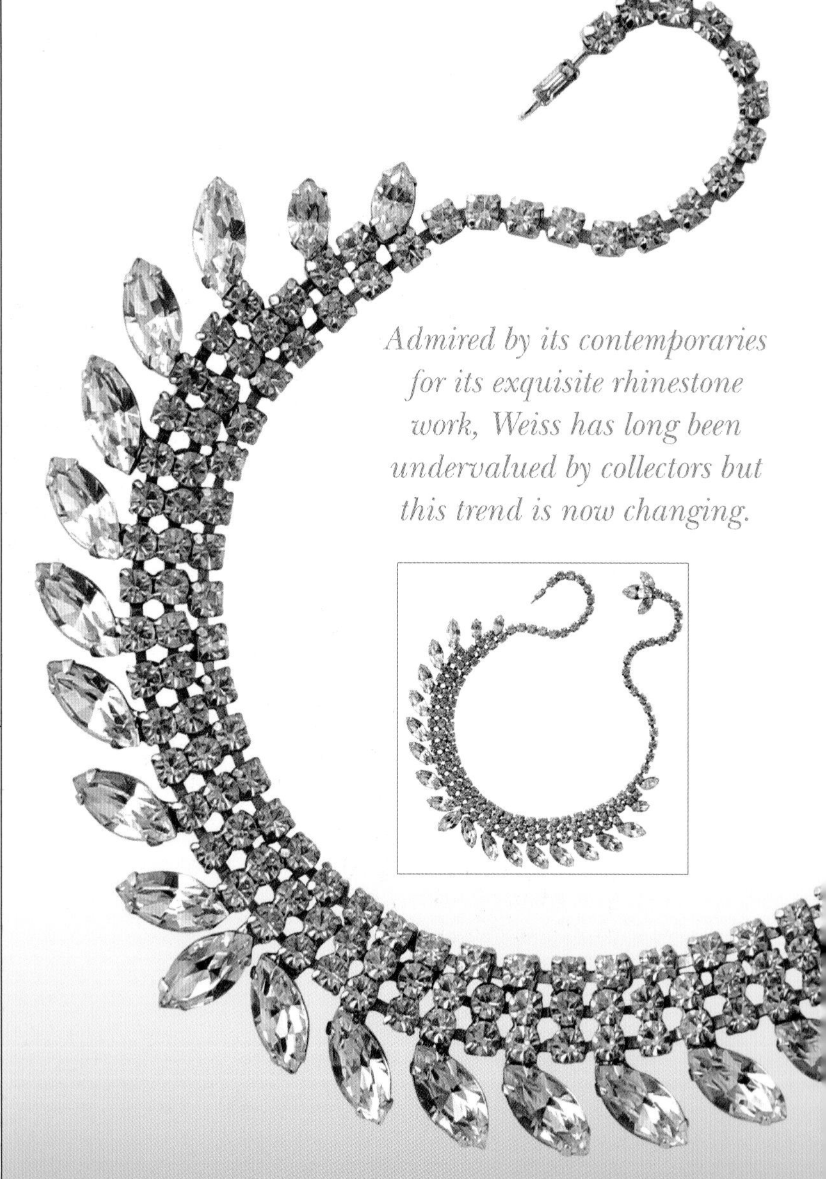

Admired by its contemporaries for its exquisite rhinestone work, Weiss has long been undervalued by collectors but this trend is now changing.

Weiss diamanté necklace with faceted oval-shaped drops. *1950s* ★★☆☆☆

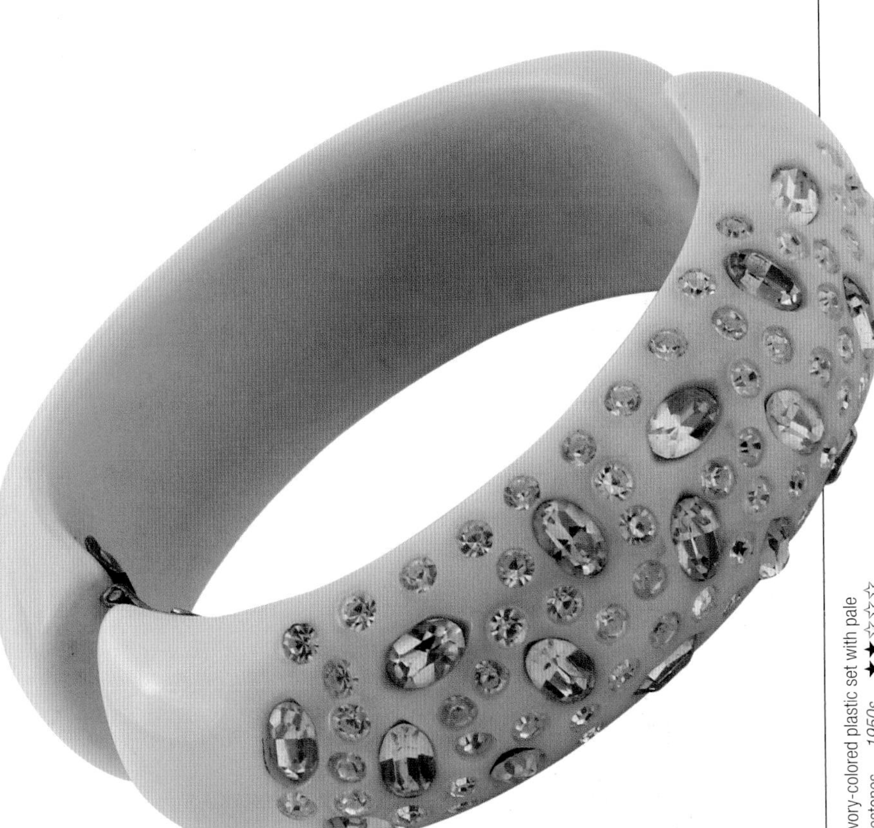

Weiss hinged bracelet in ivory-colored plastic set with pale blue and clear crystal rhinestones. *1950s* ★★☆☆☆

p.143 p.121 p.298

p.373 p.31 p.113

p.137 p.372 p.225

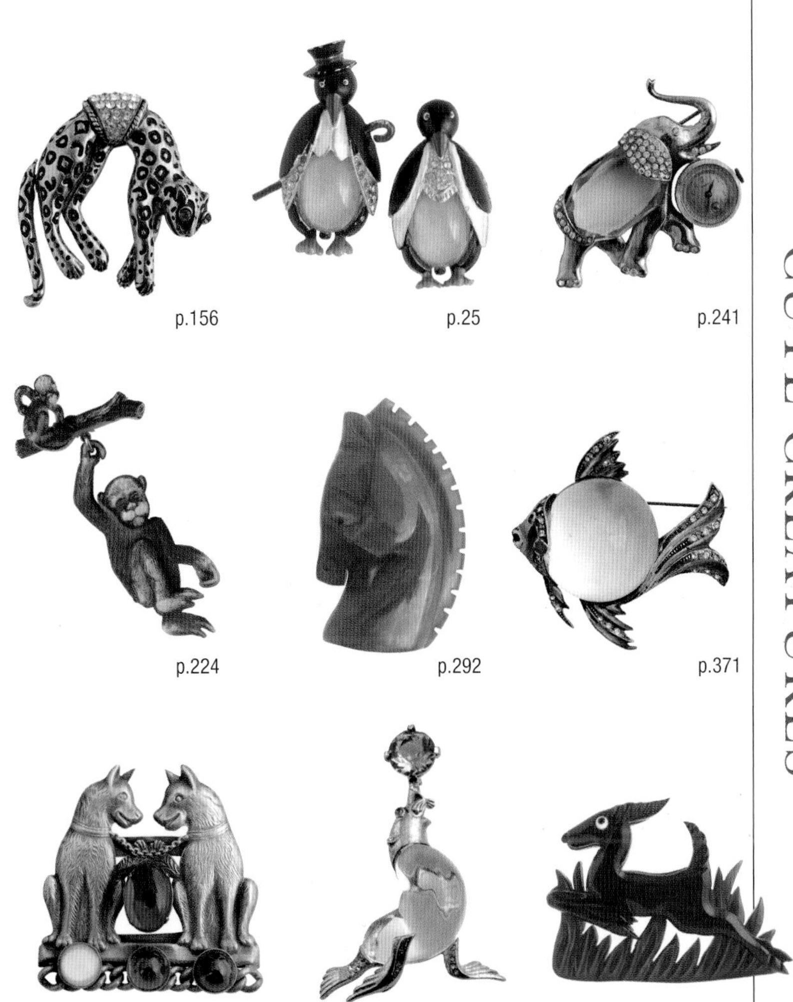

p.156 p.25 p.241

p.224 p.292 p.371

p.46 p.367 p.293

Whiting & Davis antiqued gold-plated bracelet with sections of engraved cross-hatching and applied stylized flowers and leaves. *1970s* ★☆☆☆☆

Whiting & Davis silver-plated coiled snake bangle with expandable mesh wrist band and a solid punched and engraved head. *1960s* ★☆☆☆☆

"I have always believed that fashion was not only to make women more beautiful, but also to reassure them, give them confidence."

YVES SAINT LAURENT

Yves Saint Laurent necklace with geometric motifs of gilt metal linked with twin strands of white faux pearls. *1980s* ★☆☆☆☆

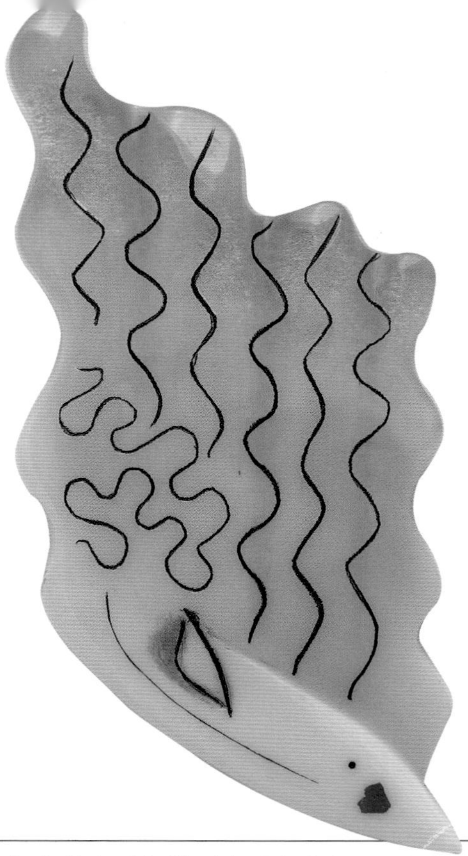

Yves Saint Laurent earrings with amethyst, aquamarine, sapphire, and amber crystal rhinestones, prong-set in gold-plated castings with turquoise and red enameling. *Late 1980s* ★★☆☆☆

Zandra Rhodes stylized female head with flowing hair pin of skin-colored plastic with black and lipstick rouge highlights. *c.1970s* ★★★☆☆

Primarily known as a fashion and textile designer, Rhodes's bold designs have been worn by high profile figures such as the late Diana, Princess of Wales.

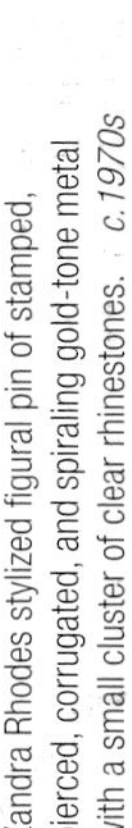

Zandra Rhodes stylized figural pin of stamped, pierced, corrugated, and spiraling gold-tone metal with a small cluster of clear rhinestones. *c.1970s*

UNSIGNED PIECES

Most costume jewelry is unsigned, and these pieces constitute a veritable Aladdin's cave of treasures. While thousands of devoted fans compete for signed pieces by the great names in fashion, some of the most interesting, beautiful, and affordable pieces are by unidentified makers. Quality is the key to value, and materials, craftsmanship, and settings should be checked carefully. Particularly popular are creature and figural pins, and pieces that strongly reflect the style of an era such as Art Deco.

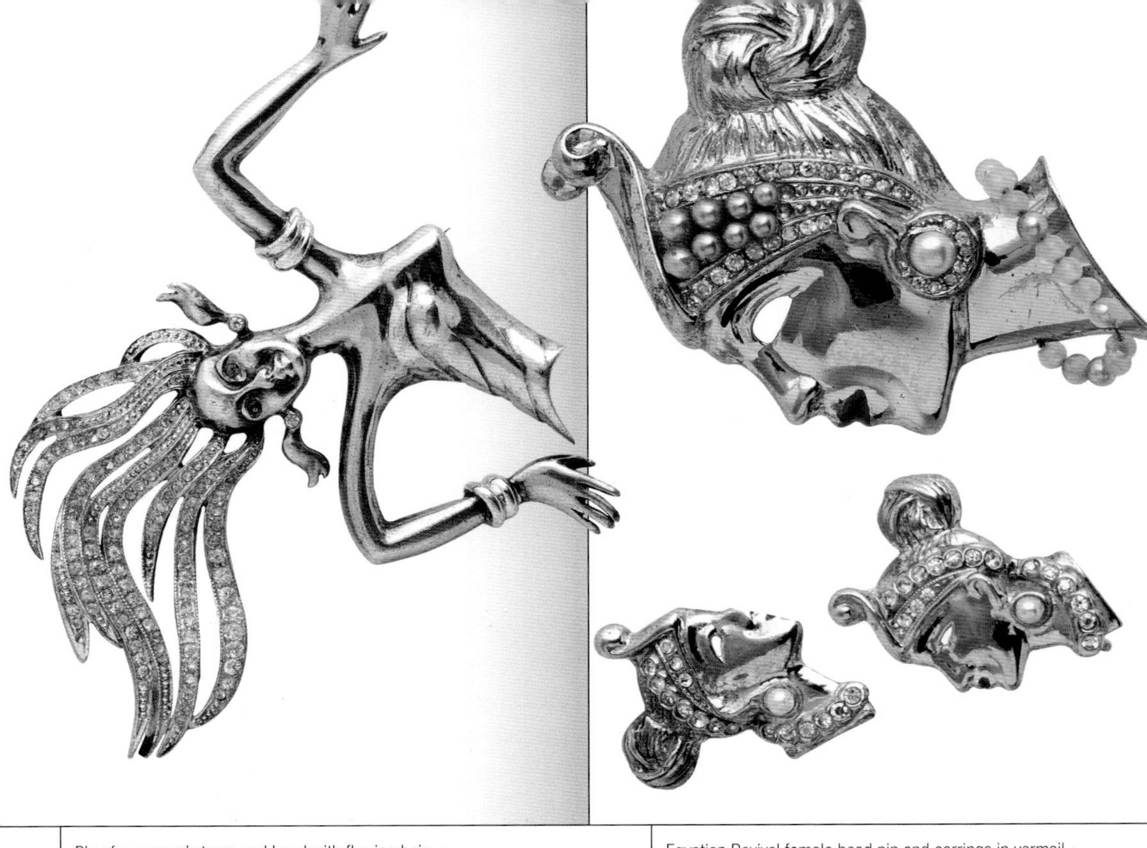

Pin of a woman's torso and head with flowing hair, in vermeil sterling silver and pavé-set clear crystal rhinestones. *1940s* ★★☆☆☆

Egyptian Revival female head pin and earrings in vermeil sterling silver with faux pearls. *1930s* ★★☆☆☆

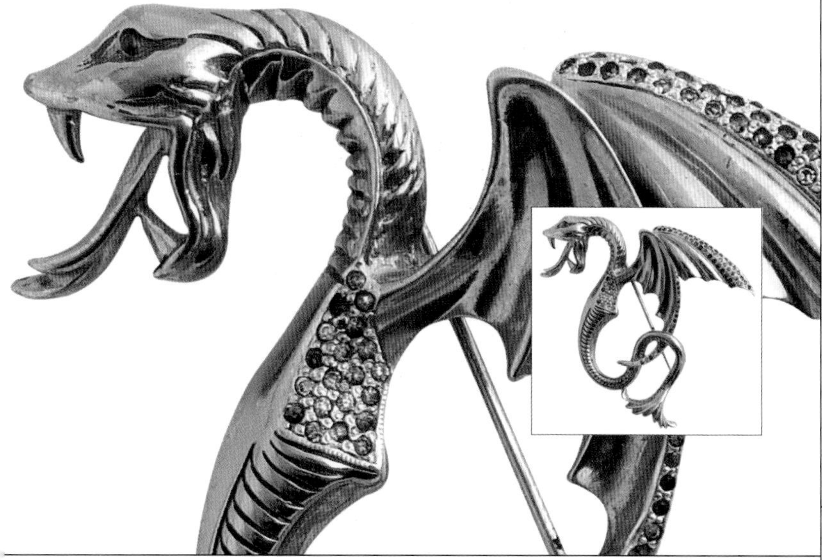

Pin in the form of a winged serpent, the body and wings of which are set with tiny diamanté. *1940s* ★★☆☆☆

Byzantine-style floral pin made of gilt metal and set with clear crystal rhinestones and faux pearls. *1960s* ★☆☆☆☆

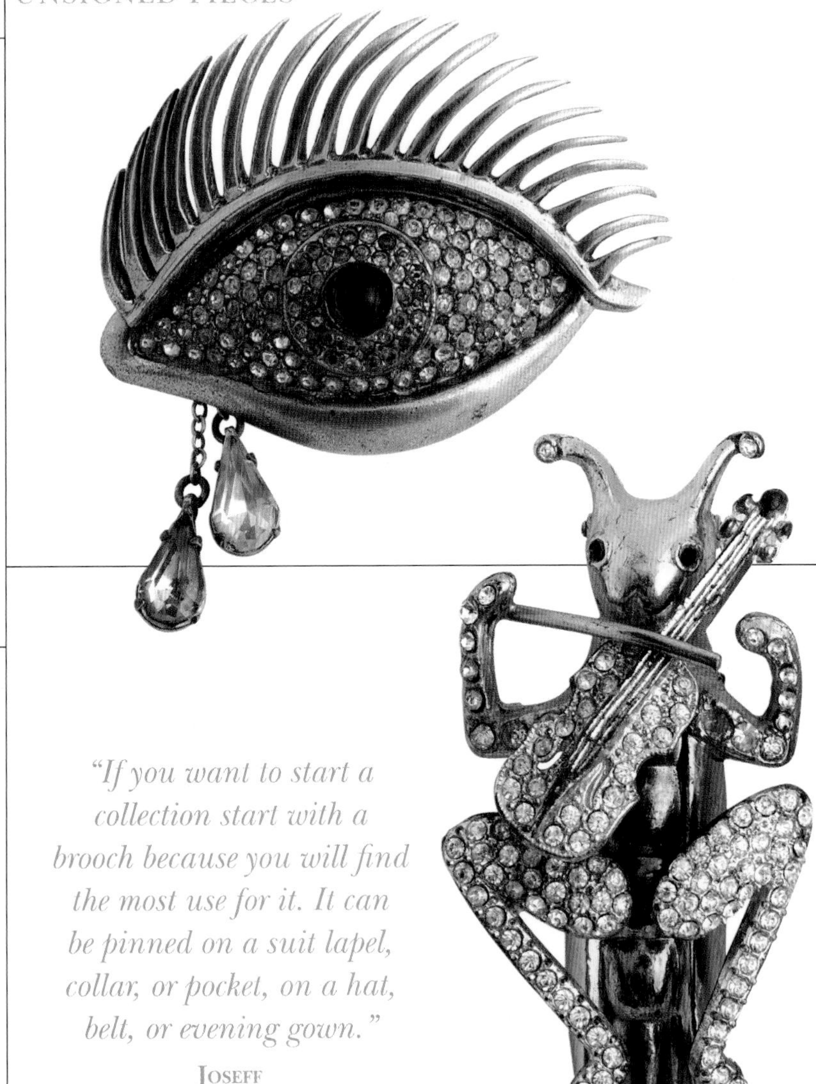

Eye pin of vermeil sterling silver with pavé-set clear and sapphire crystal rhinestones, a black glass cabochon, and two rhinestone drops. *1940s* ★★★☆☆

Cricket playing a violin pin of gold-plated metal with enameling and pavé-set clear crystal rhinestones. *1930s* ★★☆☆☆

"If you want to start a collection start with a brooch because you will find the most use for it. It can be pinned on a suit lapel, collar, or pocket, on a hat, belt, or evening gown."

JOSEFF

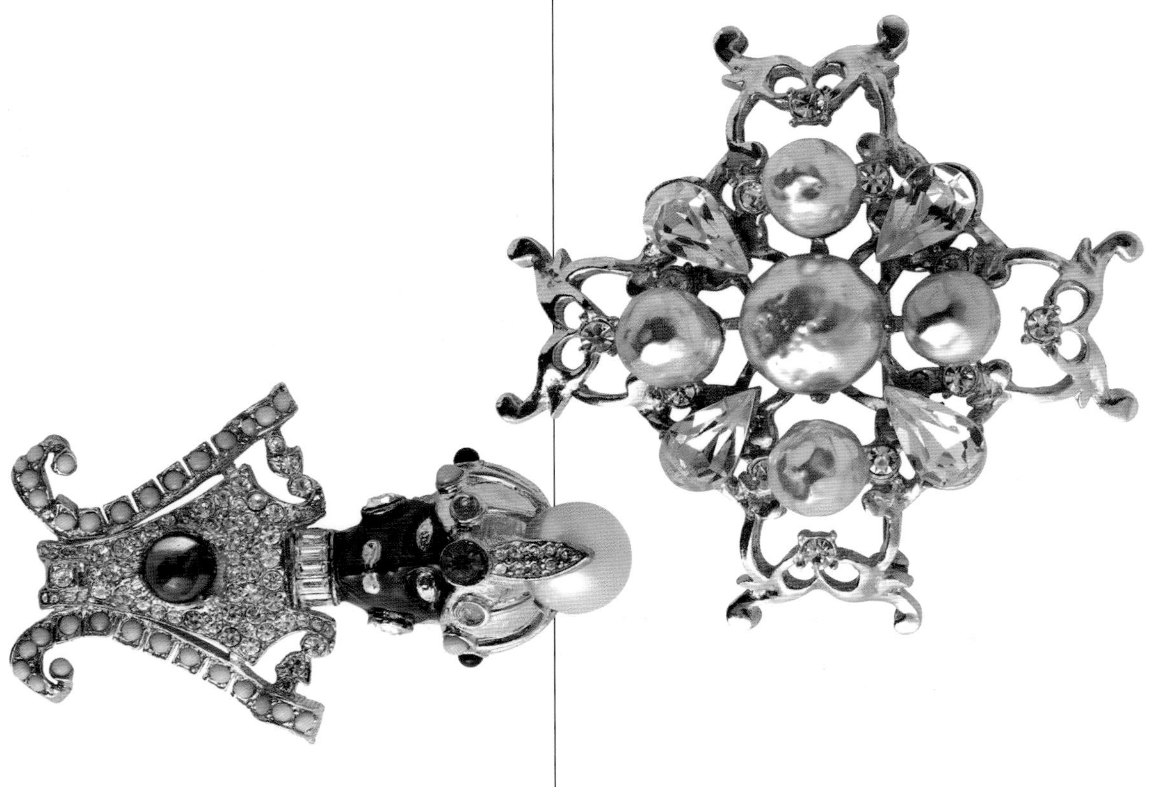

Caliph pin of gold-tone metal casting with black enameling, aquamarine and turquoise glass cabochons, clear rhinestones, and a faux pearl. *1960s* ★★☆☆☆

Maltese Cross pin with scrolls of filigree gold wire set with faux baroque pearls and clear rhinestones. *1960s* ★☆☆☆☆

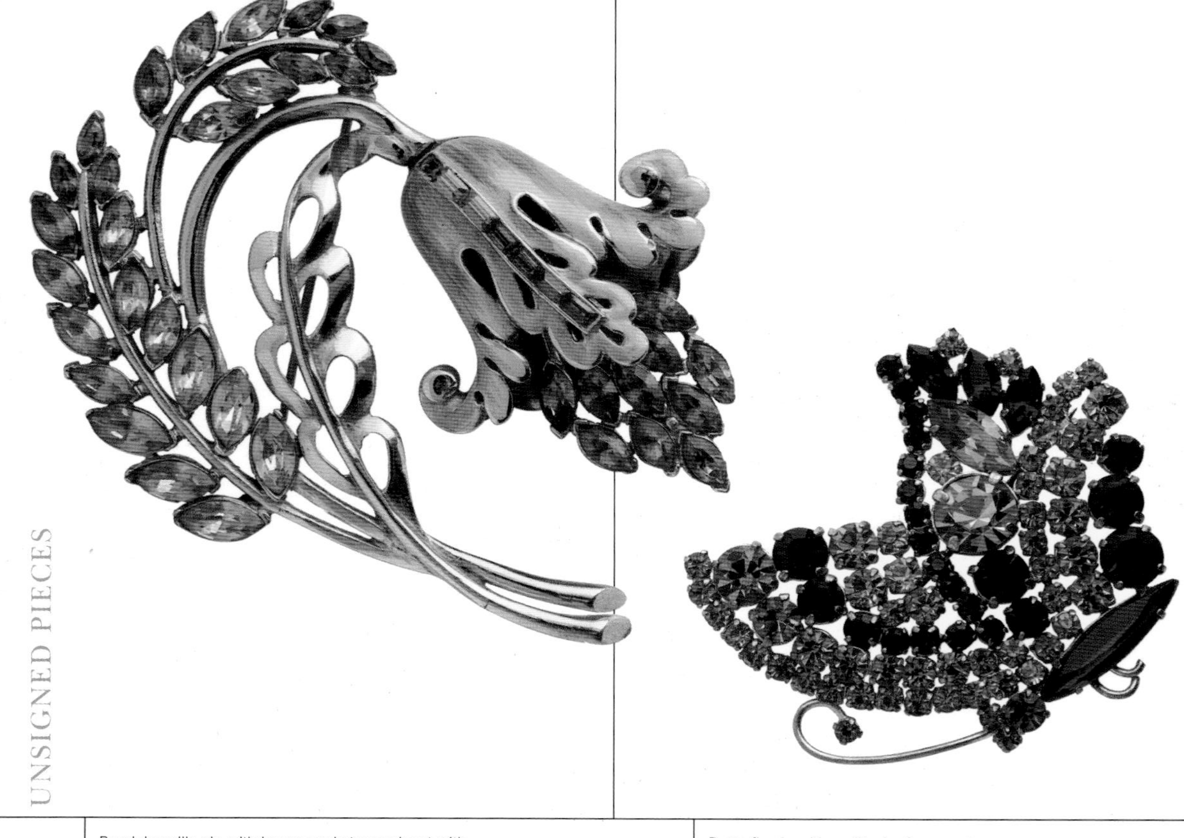

Pendulous lily pin with leaves and stamen inset with pink-faceted diamanté, and the enameled flower studded with baguette-cut diamanté. *1940s* ★★☆☆☆

Butterfly pin with a gilt wire frame set with pink, mauve, ruby red, and green rhinestones. *1950s* ★☆☆☆☆

Unmarked brooch with clusters of differently shaped faceted stones in shades of pink. *1950s* ★★☆☆☆

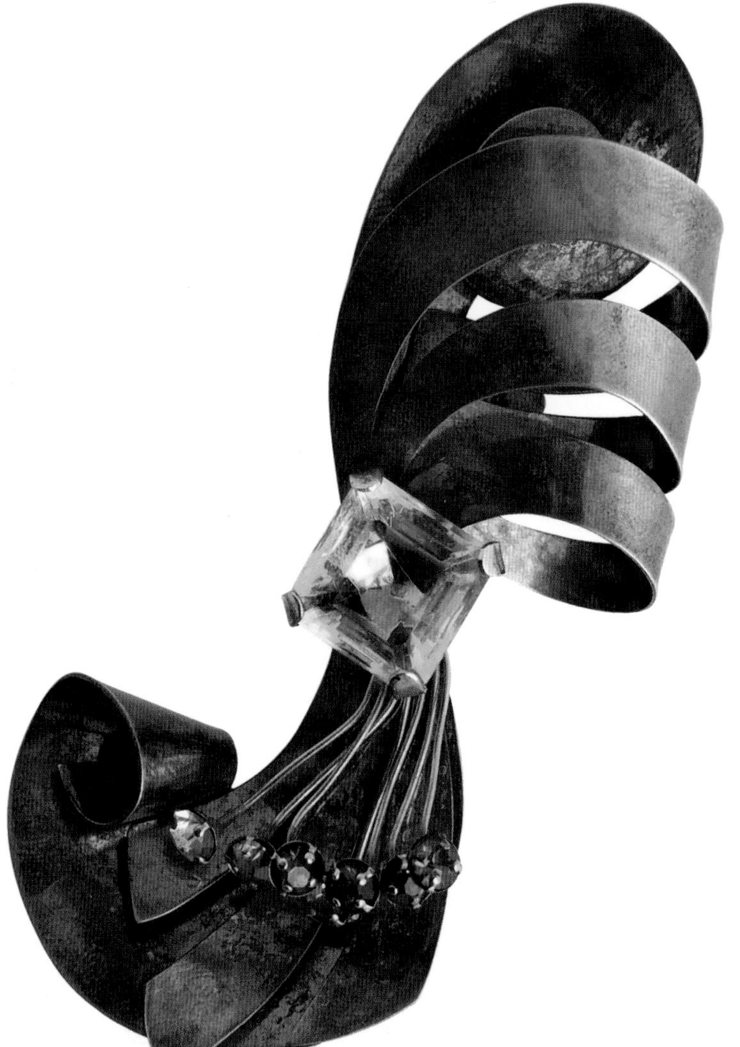

Musical clef pin of vermeil sterling silver with a large central aquamarine paste and emerald, sapphire, ruby, and aquamarine crystal rhinestones. *1940s* ★☆☆☆☆

Unsigned peacock pin of silver-tone metal set with pavé diamanté and with a tail of clustered purple stones. ★★★☆

"I adore wearing gems, but not because they are mine. You can't possess radiance, you can only admire it."

Elizabeth Taylor

p.332 p.341 p.247

p.135 p.202 p.11

p.253 p.65 p.193

p.130
p.182
p.203
p.42
p.285
p.324
p.269
p.192
p.129

Continental silver and paste basket brooch; marked "835". *1930s* ★★★☆☆

English silver and paste floral brooch; marked "sterling silver". *1920s* ★★☆☆☆

Pin in the shape of a vase of flowers created with faceted ruby, emerald, and apple green glass stones, and clear crystal rhinestones. *1940s* ★★★☆☆

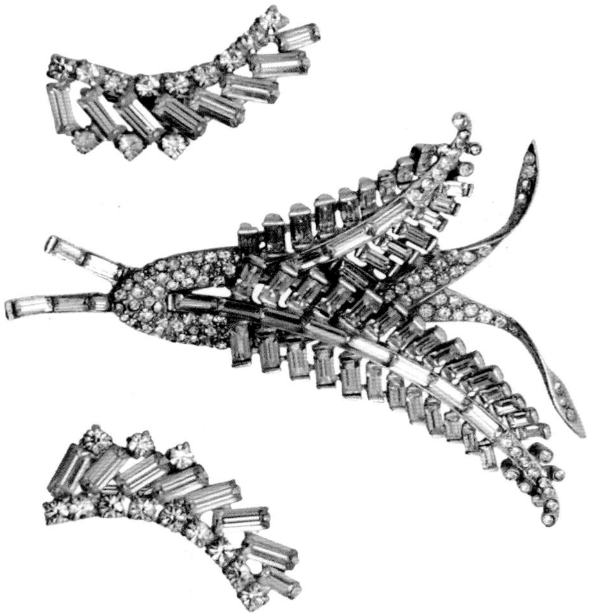

Pin and earrings of stylized leaf form in sterling-silver set with round- and baguette-cut clear crystal rhinestones. *1940s* ★★☆☆☆

Basket of flowers pin with green and coral Lucite petals and leaves, and clear crystal rhinestones.
Late 1930s ★★☆☆☆

"Accessories are important and becoming more and more important every day."

Giorgio Armani

Basket of flowers pin set with channel-cut ruby and pavé crystals. *1930s* ★★★☆☆

Bonsai tree pin, the branches of which are set with multicolored diamanté, enamel flowers, and leaves. *1950s* ★★☆☆☆

Tree pin with enameled leaves and flowers, applied faux pearls, and inset diamanté. *1950s* ★★☆☆☆

Ballerina pin and earrings in vermeil sterling silver with faceted aquamarine and sapphire glass stones, and clear crystal rhinestones. *1940s* ★★★☆☆

Ballroom dancer pin in vermeil sterling silver with black enameling and faux sapphires, emeralds, and ruby baguettes. *1940s* ★★★☆☆

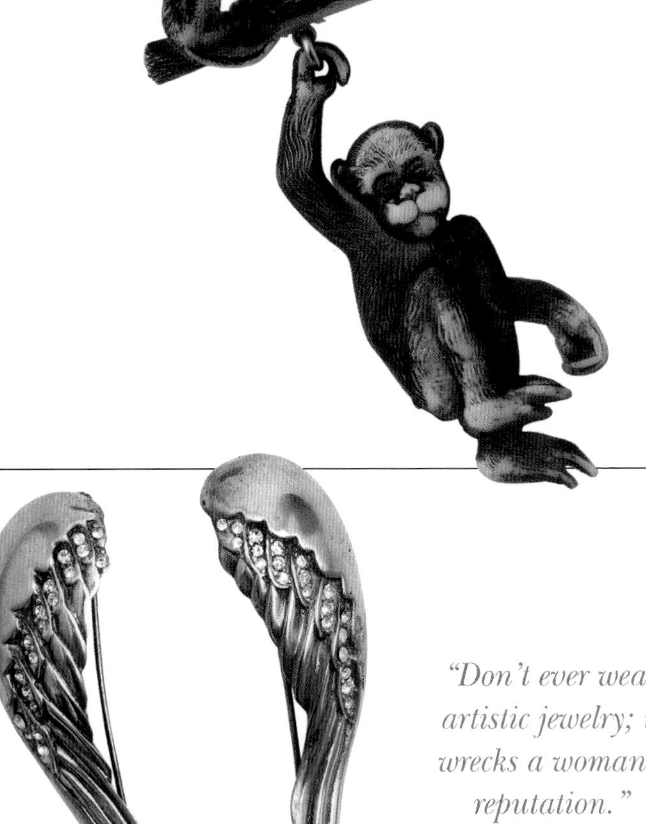

Swinging brown monkey pin, with a baby monkey on a branch above. *1930s* ★☆☆☆☆

Pair of American sterling-silver and gold-plated wing brooches. *1940s* ★★☆☆☆

"Don't ever wear artistic jewelry; it wrecks a woman's reputation."

COLETTE

Victorian kingfisher pin made of carved horn with a pearlized finish. *c.1900* ★★☆☆☆

American cartoon cow fur clip, unmarked but bearing a patent number. *1930s* ★★★★☆

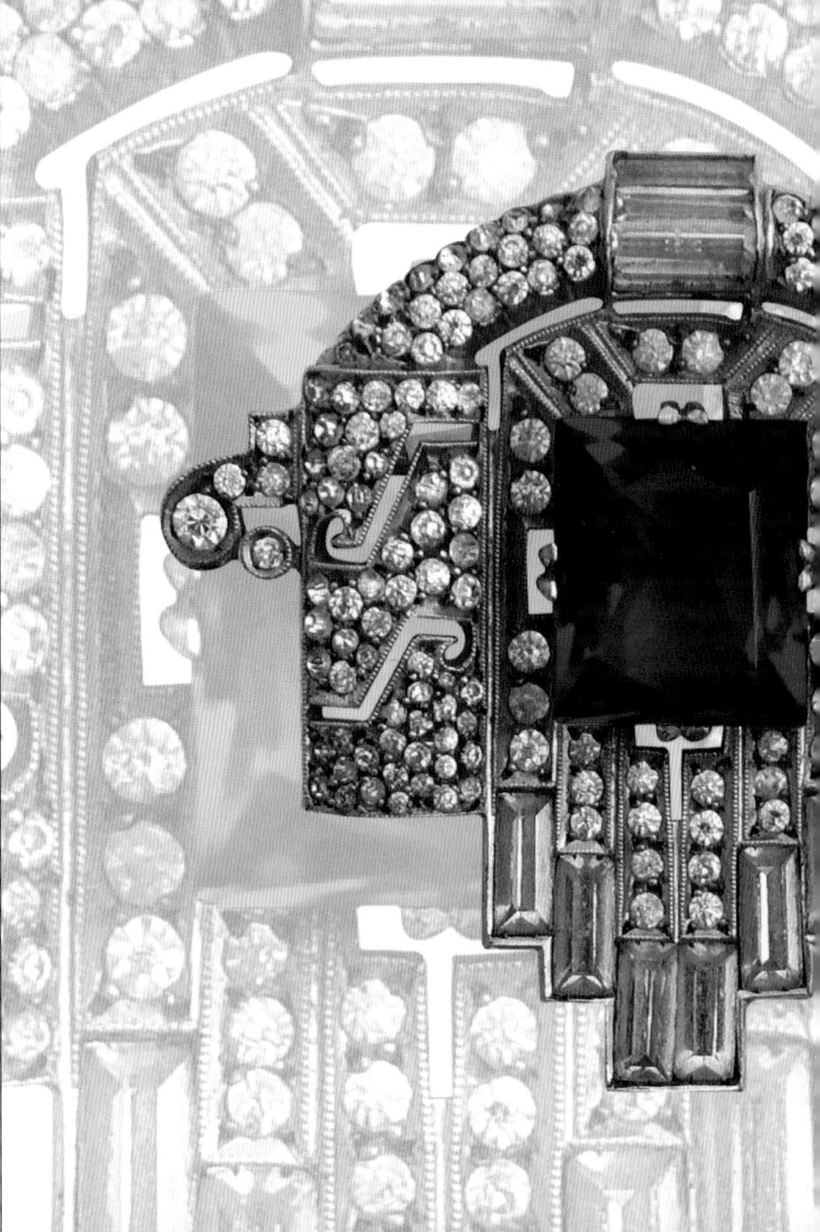

ART DECO JEWELRY

The era that oozed glamour and sophistication gave us some of the most stylish and desirable jewelry of the 20th century. Whether made from Bakelite, glass beads, or real diamonds, Art Deco jewelry, with its geometrical forms and bold colors, reflects the optimism and excitement of the post-World War I era. Turning their backs on the sinuous lines of the Art Nouveau period, designers of the 1920s and 30s worked with radical new forms influenced by the sleek lines of the Machine Age, the Modernist architecture of skyscrapers, and the Cubist and Futurist art movements. Decoration took inspiration from recently discovered Egyptian and Aztec styles, while new materials such as plastics enabled exciting experimentation in design.

Unmarked English silver and paste Art Deco brooch in rhodium-plated silver with a red central stone. *1930s* ★★☆☆☆

"Fashion is made to become unfashionable."

COCO CHANEL

American sterling-silver and gold-plated blackamoor clip, the black glass face set with clear rhinestones. ★★☆☆☆

Enameled silver blackamoor pin with green and red diamanté and a faux pearl. *1940s* ★★☆☆☆

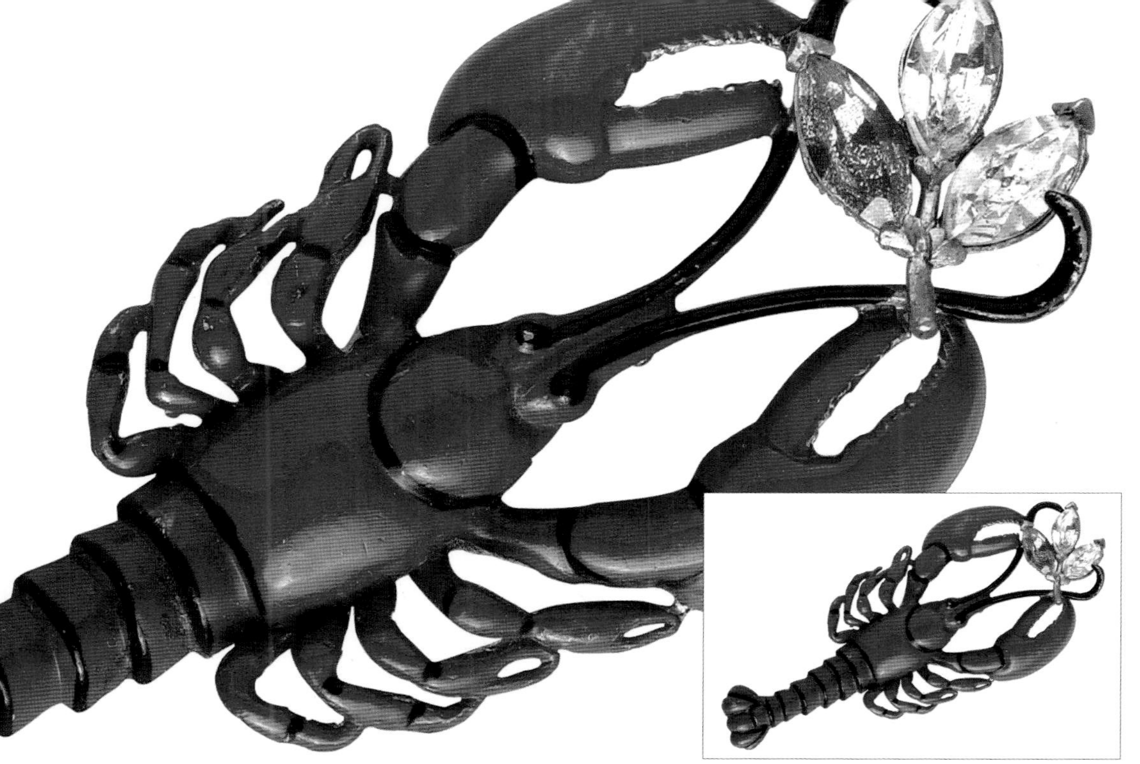

Red enameled lobster pin with painted details and claws holding faceted glass stones. ★★☆☆☆

French brooch in rhodium-plated silver with prong-set fruit salad stones. *1930s* ★★★★☆

The "fruit salad" style was inspired by the Indian Moghul "Tree of Life" jewels. Instead of being faceted, stones were carved to resemble fruit and leaves.

American brooch in rhodium-plated silver with prong-set fruit salad stones. *1930s* ★★★★☆

Pin of abstract design with silver-set amber and citrine-faceted pastes and cabochons. *1920s* ★★★★☆

Edwardian circular flower motif pin, gold-plated with red, blue, green, amber, and clear crystal rhinestones. ★★☆☆☆

Large American circular fruit salad pin. *1930s* ★★☆☆☆

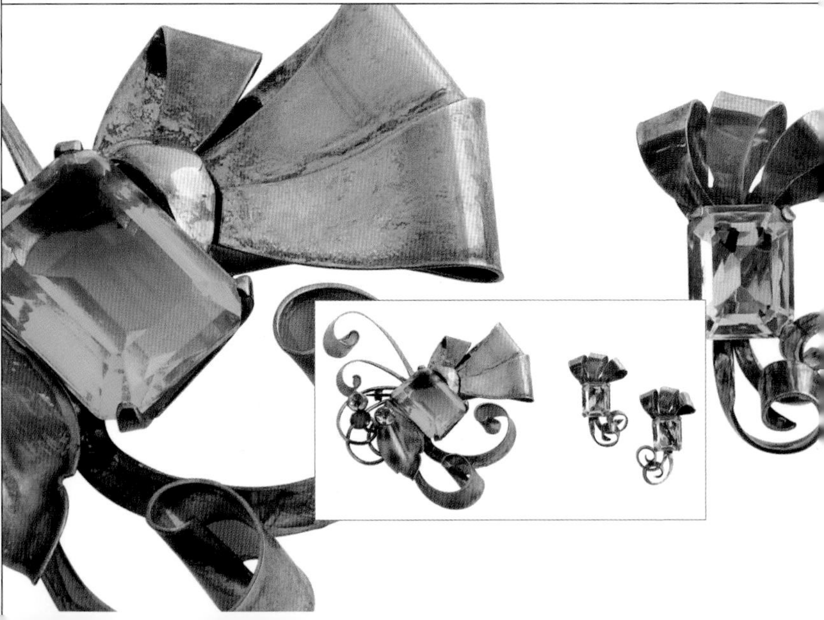

Set of aquamarine, ruby, and jonquil earrings and pin. *1940s* ★★☆☆☆

Moorish-style pin of antiqued gilt metal with a large faux amethyst, turquoise and pale blue glass cabochons, and white, red, turquoise, and black enamel. *1920s* ★★☆☆☆

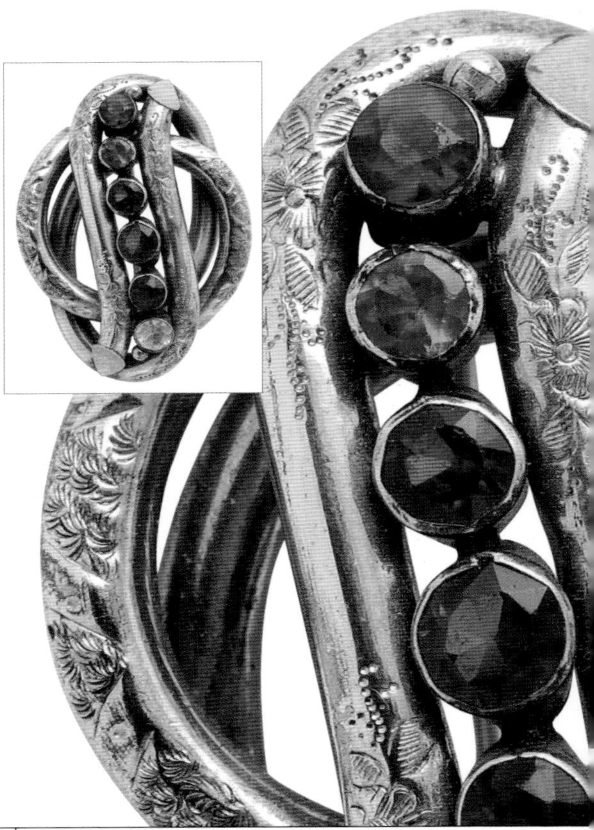

Victorian love knot "Regard" pin decorated with faux ruby, emerald, garnet, amethyst, ruby, and diamond. *c.1860* ★★★★☆

Bush pin and earrings with carved lime green Lucite leaves and prong-set round- and navette-cut rhinestones on gold-tone backs. *Late 1950s* ★★☆☆☆

Floral motif pin and earrings with aquamarine crystal rhinestones and dark blue glass cabochons, prong-set in gilt wire backs. *1950s* ★★☆☆☆

Entwined snakes pin in brass with a large jade green plastic stone and four jade green drops. *1915–20* ★★☆☆☆

Zebra pin-pendant of vermeil sterling silver with black enameling, clear crystal rhinestones, and an emerald glass cabochon. *1940s* ★★☆☆☆

Flower pin with open and close "night-and-day" mechanism, of gilt metal with blue enameling and clear crystal rhinestones. *1950s* ★★☆☆☆

Art Deco amethyst glass and marcasite brooch. *c.1925* ★☆☆☆☆

BEAUTIFUL BUNCHES

p.219 p.95 p.185

p.181 p.94 p.126

p.76 p.158 p.178

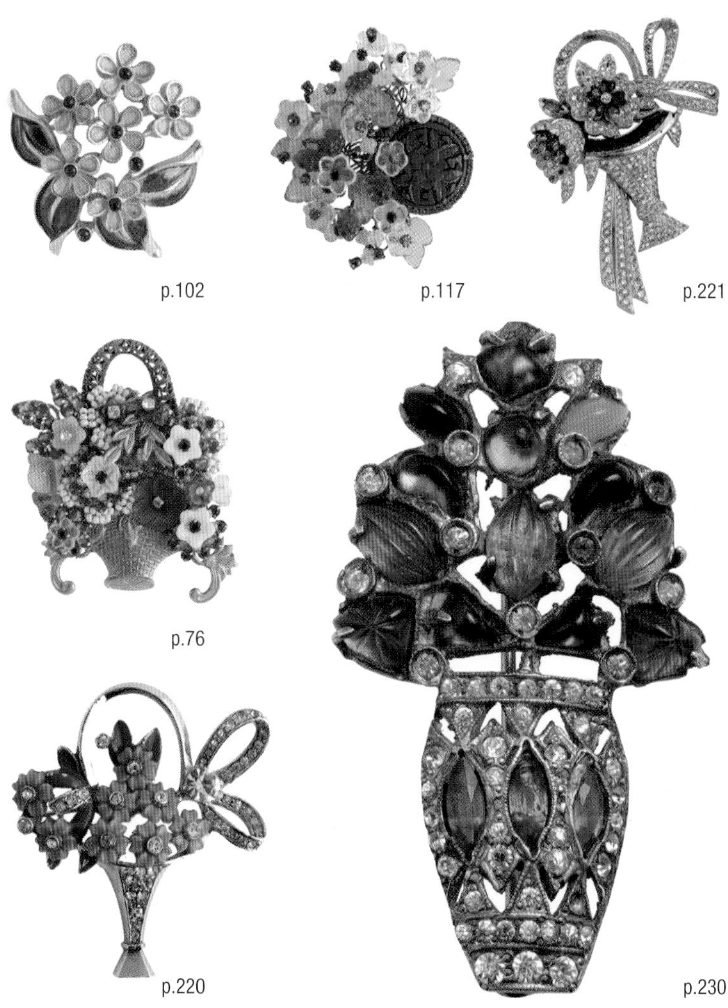

p.102

p.117

p.221

p.76

p.220

p.230

American blackamoor pin with black enameled head and gold-plated turban. *1940s* ★★★★☆

Heart-shaped brooch and earrings in poured glass. *1920s* ★★☆☆☆

Elephant watch pin in vermeil sterling-silver, with faceted glass faux sapphire body and clear crystal rhinestones. *1940s* ★★☆☆☆

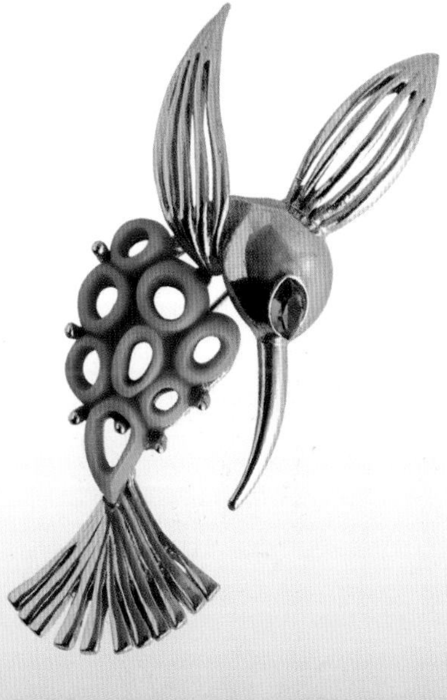

Stylized humming bird pin of gold-plated metal set with turquoise Lucite rings and aquamarine crystal rhinestone eyes. *1960s* ★☆☆☆☆

"I like to collect costume jewelry. It's better designed and has more character than high-end jewelry."

IMAN

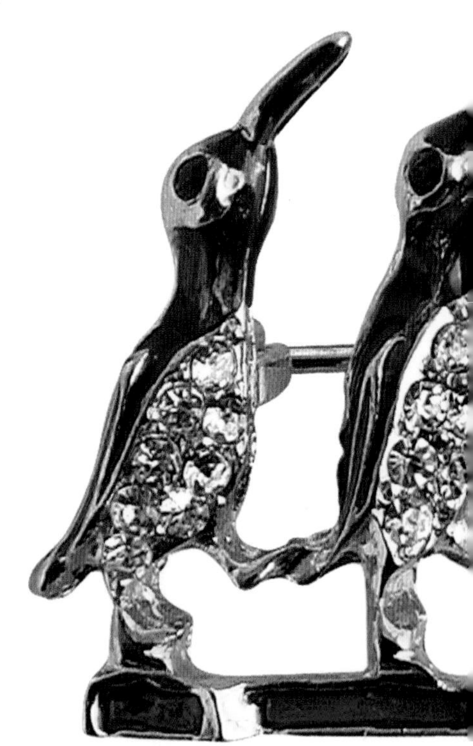

Penguins pin showing a mother and two babies, decorated with brown enameling, pavé-set clear rhinestones, and green glass cabochon eyes. *1950s* ★☆☆☆☆

Bracelet of gold-plated metal with prong-set aquamarine, blue *aurora borealis* and sapphire crystal rhinestones. *1950s* ★☆☆☆☆

French silver Art Deco bracelet with round- and baguette-cut clear crystal rhinestones, emerald glass cabochons, and carved fruit salad stones. *1930s* ★★★★★

Glass clamper bracelet and earring set with white glass flowers, faux natural pearls, colored glass fruits, and diamanté-inset spheres and bars. *1960s* ★☆☆☆☆

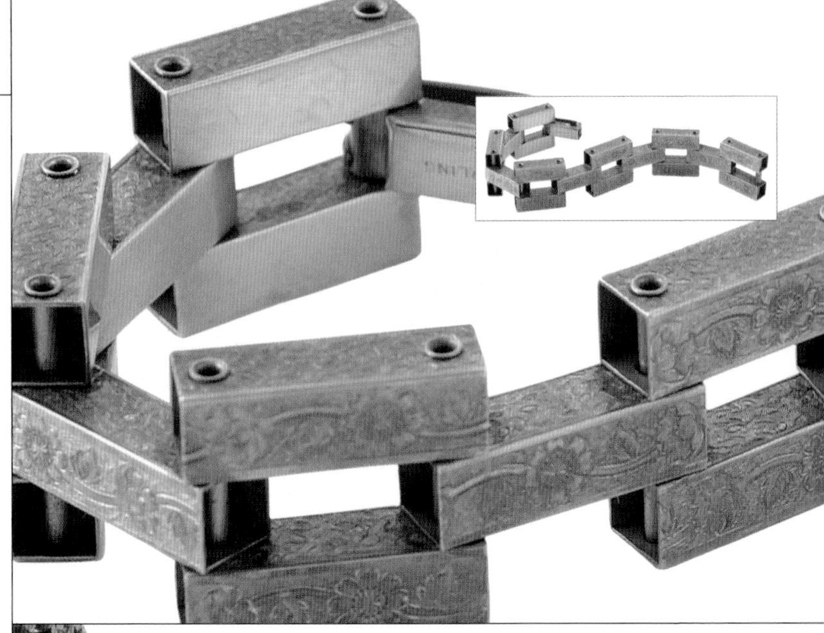

American Art Deco sterling-silver bracelet with engraved floral motifs. *1920s* ★★☆☆☆

Bracelet with gold-plated clasp and link, and round-cut rose pink crystal rhinestones. *1950s* ★★☆☆☆

Glass and diamanté-inset bracelet; possibly a copy of a David Webb piece. *1940s* ★★★★★

Victorian woven horsehair bracelet with a gilt metal clasp engraved with a floral motif. *c.1840* ★★★☆☆

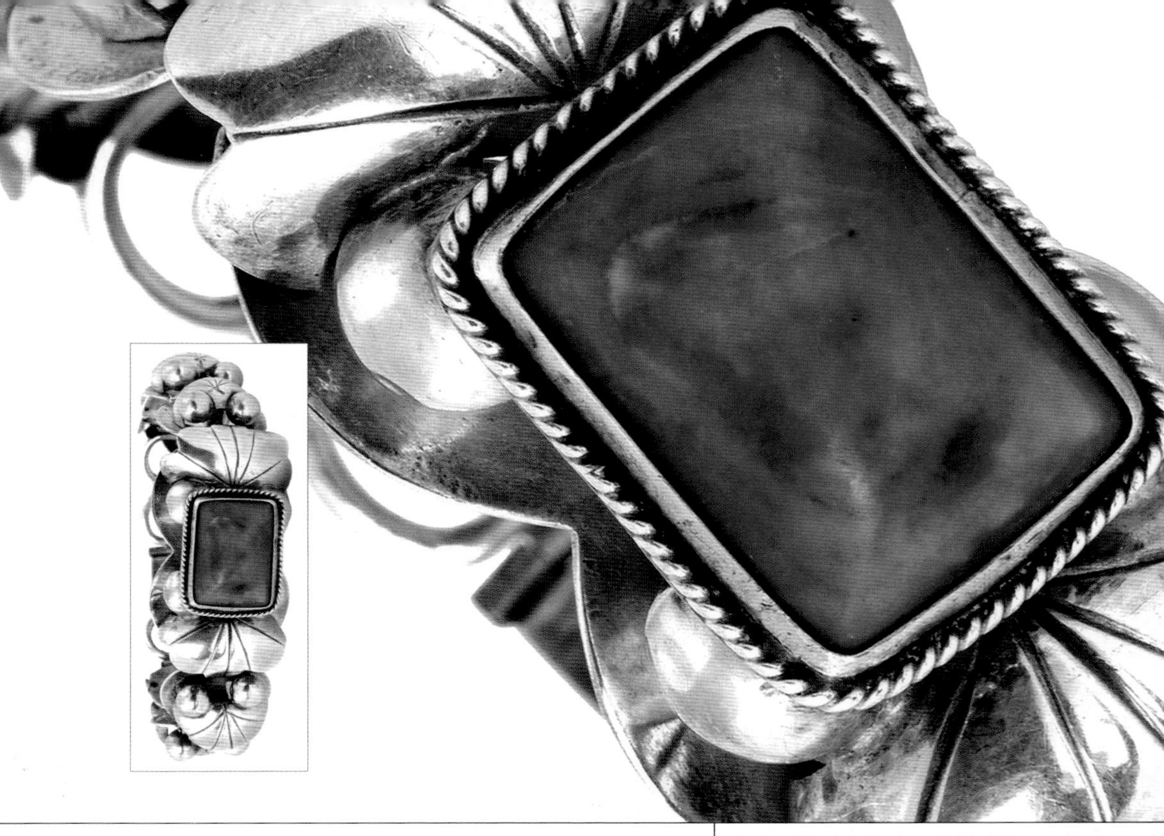

Mexican silver bracelet formed of leaf shapes with a central green stone. *c.1940* ★★★☆☆

Silver bracelet set with three faceted, emerald green crystal stones. *1920s* ★★☆☆☆

Unmarked cocktail bracelet decorated with scenes from the opera *The Marriage of Figaro*. *1940s* ★★★★★

Bracelet in japanned black metal with opaque white glass flowers and clear rhinestone. *1950s* ★★☆☆☆

"It takes all the fun out of a bracelet if you have to buy it yourself."

PEGGY JOYCE

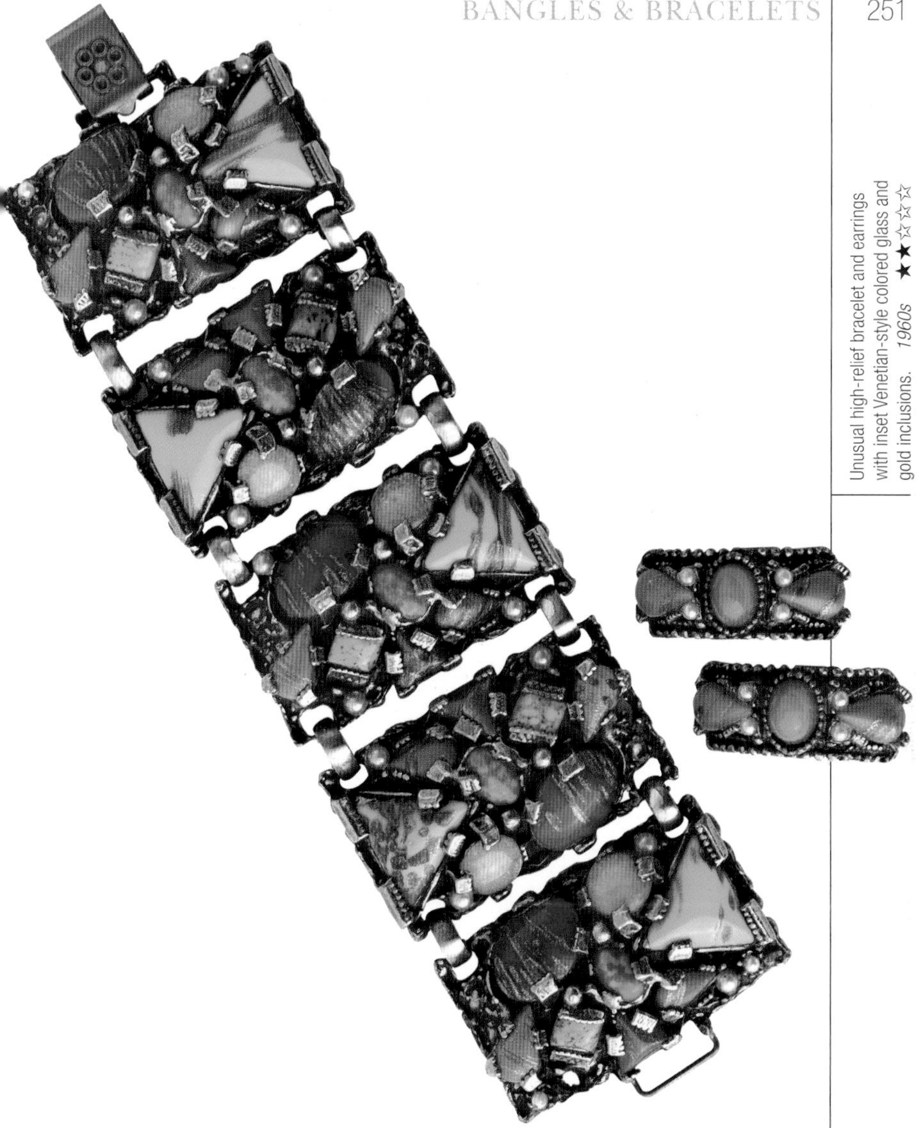

Unusual high-relief bracelet and earrings with inset Venetian-style colored glass and gold inclusions. *1960s* ★★☆☆☆

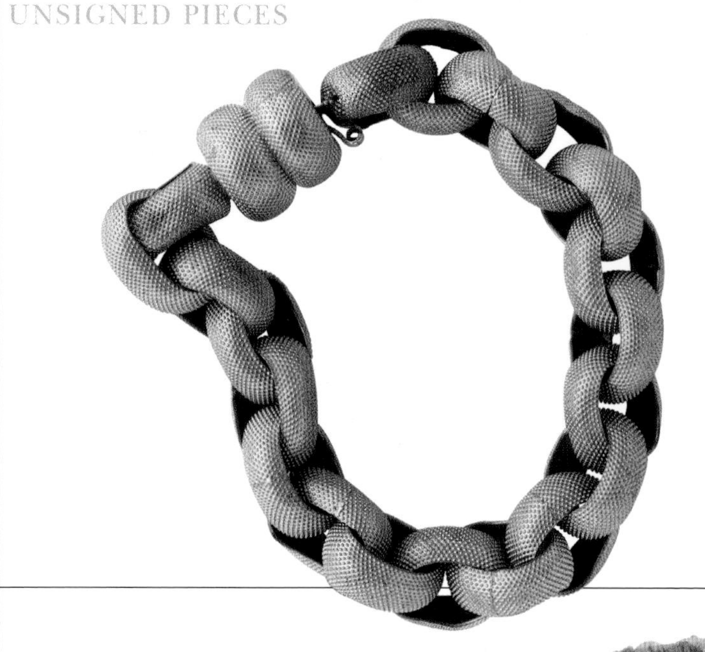

Pinchbeck bracelet with oval links and a barrell clasp. *c.1770* ★★★★☆

Expandable bracelet in textured gold-tone metal set with emerald green, ruby red, and clear crystal rhinestones. *1950s* ★★☆☆☆

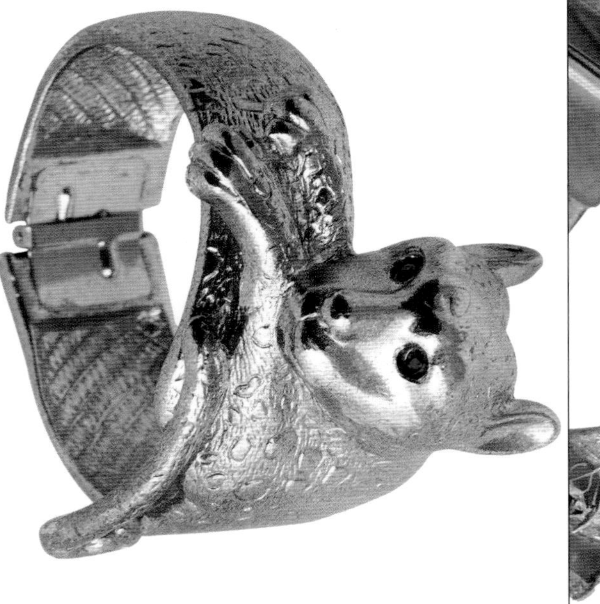

Squirrel bracelet in textured gold-tone metal with ruby red rhinestone eyes. It was probably made by Sphinx for Saks of Fifth Avenue, New York. *1980s* ★☆☆☆☆

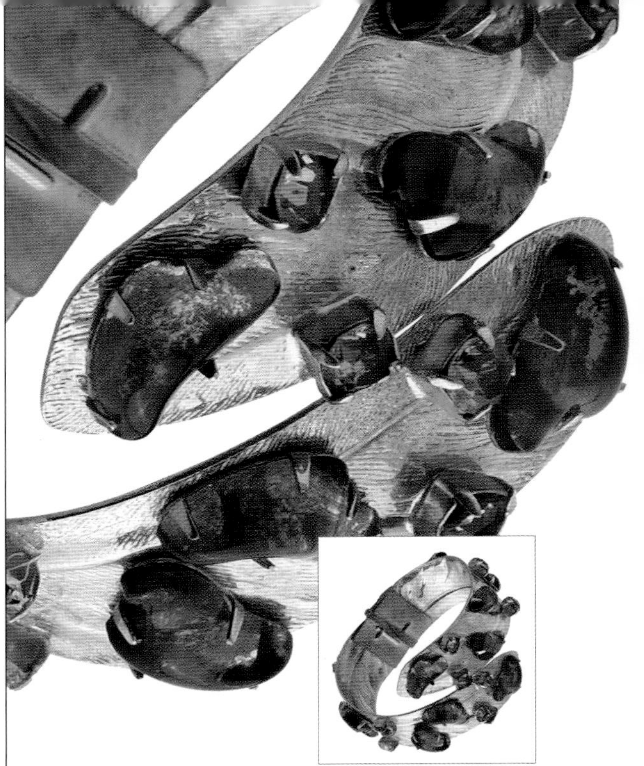

Pop Art open bangle of gold-tone metal set with citrine rhinestones and irregular lumps of smokey quartz. *Early 1970s* ★☆☆☆☆

"The pearl is the queen of gems and the gem of queens."

ANON

Floral motif necklace and earrings of vermeil sterling silver set with faux pearls. *1940s* ★☆☆☆☆

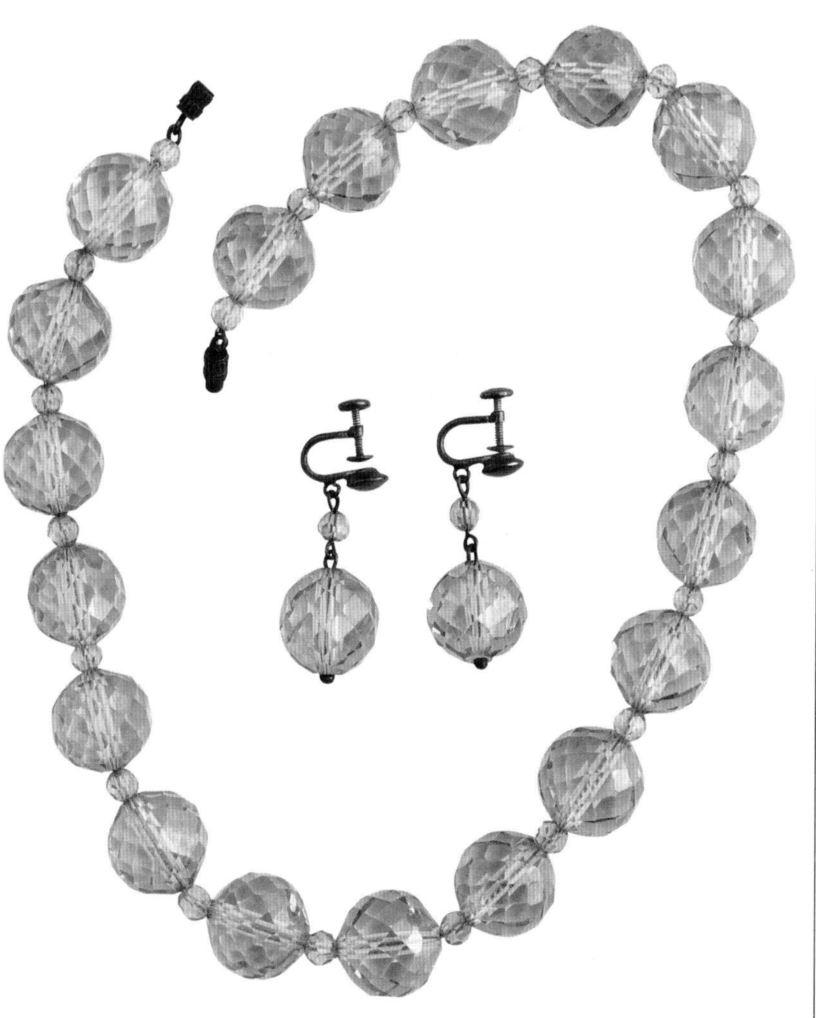

Necklace and pendant earrings with faceted rock crystal beads and drops, and small rock crystal spacers. *1930s* ★★☆☆☆

Gilt metal snake necklace inset with faceted faux amethyst and faux sapphire eyes. The head unscrews to allow fitting. *1920s* ★★★☆☆

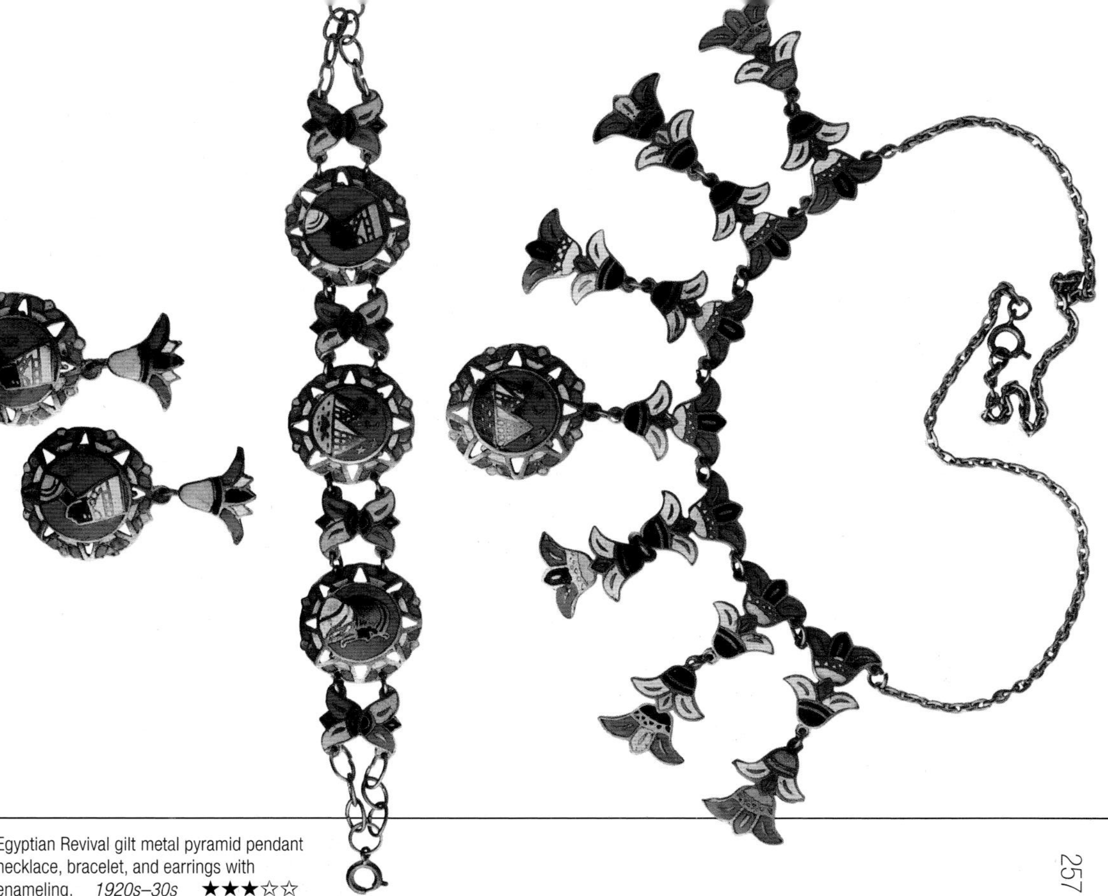

Egyptian Revival gilt metal pyramid pendant necklace, bracelet, and earrings with enameling. *1920s–30s* ★★★☆☆

Necklace and bracelet of gilt metal with peridot green rhinestones, glass cabochons, and drops. *Mid-1950s* ★★☆☆☆

Murano glass necklace with alternating oval, clear, and opaque blue glass beads. *1920s* ★★★☆☆

"Style is the dress of thoughts."

LORD CHESTERFIELD

Necklace with twin strands of faceted gray blue glass beads and a flower of gilt metal with pink glass petals and faux pearls. *1960s* ★★★☆☆

Four-strand necklace and floral motif pendant earrings with frosted citrine, olivine, and gold glass beads. The bow and hoops are strung from coral-colored cords. *1950s* ★★★☆☆

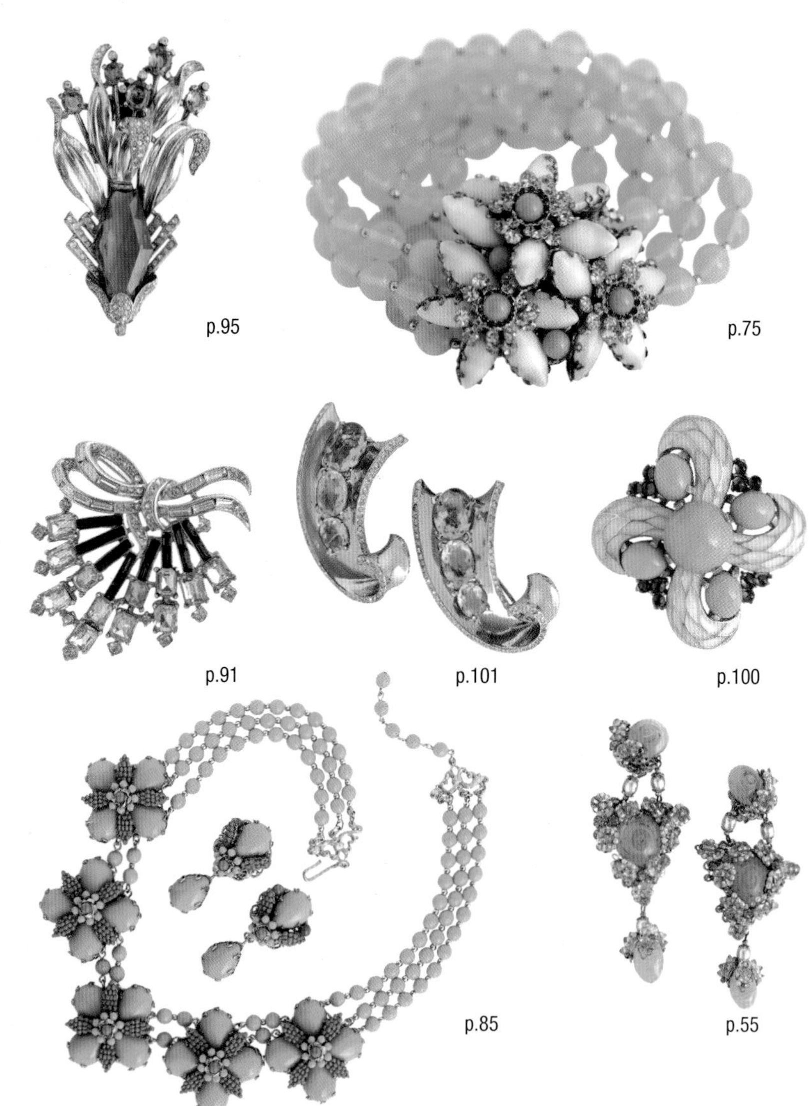

p.95

p.75

p.91

p.101

p.100

p.85

p.55

PRETTY PASTELS

p.183

p.77

p.105

p.82

p.64

p.185

p.241

p.212

Multiple-pendant necklace and earrings with inlaid gold and silver piqué. *Mid-19th century* ★★★★★

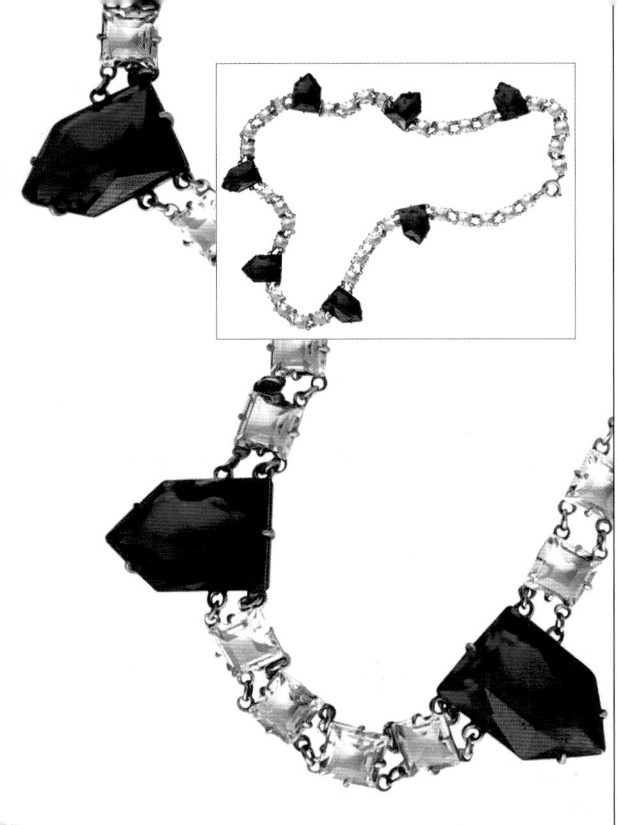

Necklace with bunches of grapes made of ruby red glass beads alternated with hoops of clear glass. *1920s* ★★☆☆☆

Necklace with silver links set with clear crystal rhinestones and faceted ruby glass shield motifs. *1920s–30s.* ★★☆☆☆

"My husband gave me a necklace. It's fake. I requested fake. Maybe I'm paranoid, but in this day and age, I don't want something around my neck that's worth more than my head."

Rita Rudner

Husks of wheat motif necklace with green, red, turquoise, black, and beige glass beads. *1930s* ★★☆☆☆

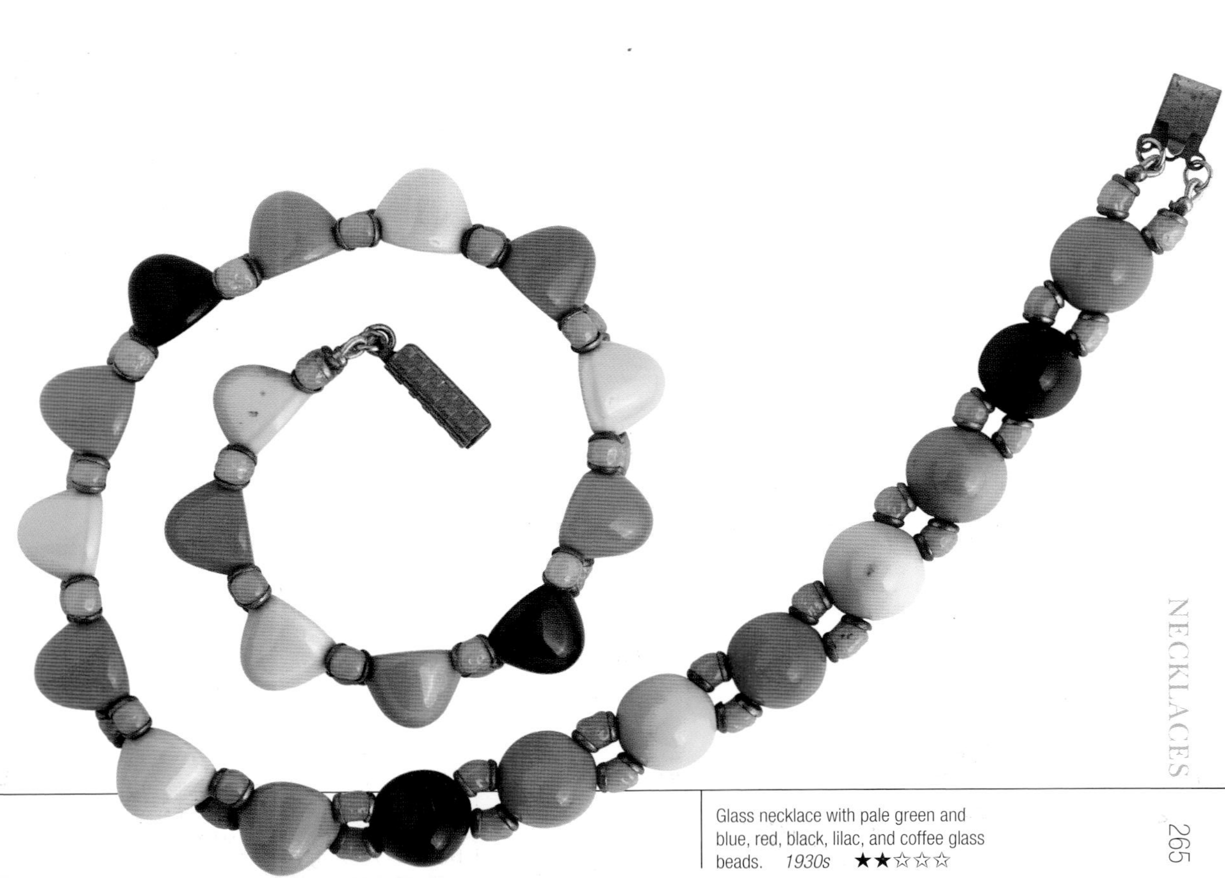

Glass necklace with pale green and blue, red, black, lilac, and coffee glass beads. *1930s* ★★☆☆☆

Pendant necklace and earrings of gold-plated metal with mottled green glass cabochons. *1960s–70s* ★★☆☆☆

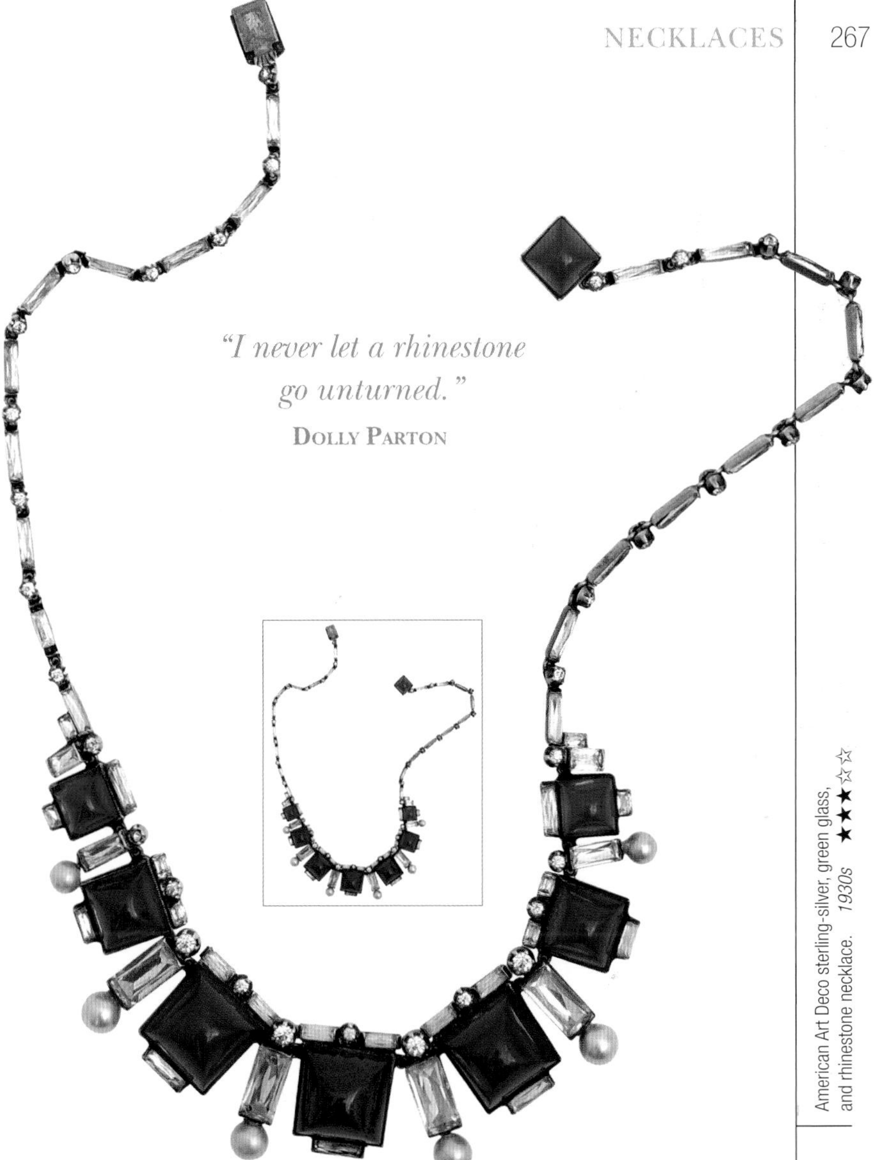

"I never let a rhinestone go unturned."

Dolly Parton

American Art Deco sterling-silver, green glass, and rhinestone necklace. *1930s* ★★★☆☆

Austrian lariat necklace with woven ropes of jet and white glass beads. *1950s* ★★★★☆

"Jewelry takes people's minds off your wrinkles."

SONJA HENIE

Mariner's Art nut necklace, lacquered and carved with floral and foliate motifs. *c.1840* ★★★★★

Pendant necklace, attributed to Rousselet, with cranberry colored glass beads and clusters of faux pearls. *1930s* ★★★★☆

American Art Deco back necklace; marked "sterling". *1930s* ★★★★☆

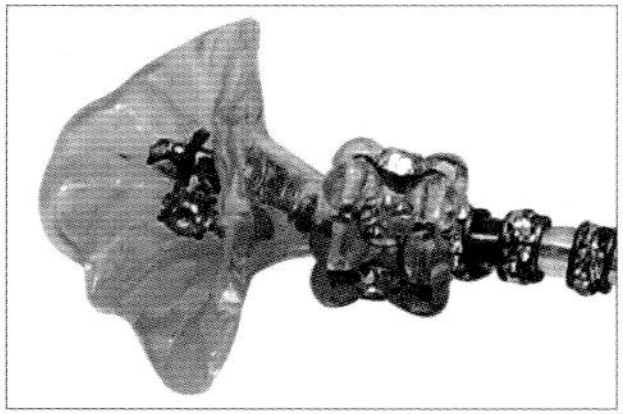

Floral motif necklace with clear Lucite links and drops, and clusters of clear crystal rhinestones. *1950s* ★★★★☆

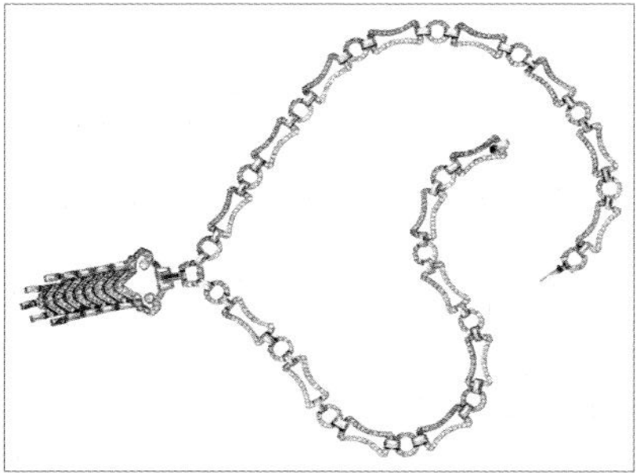

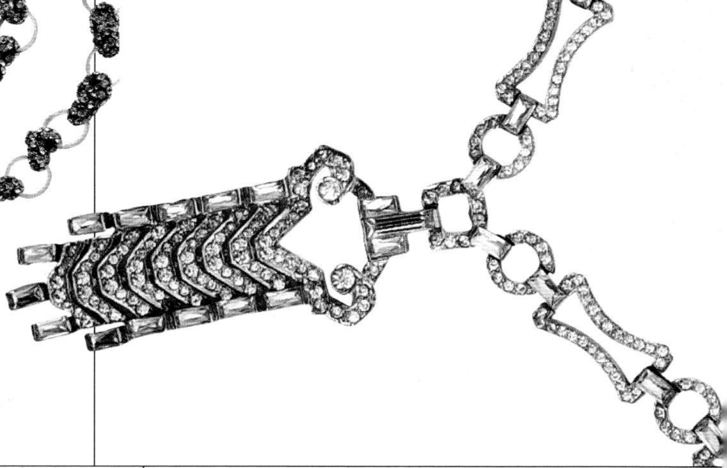

English Art Deco silver and paste necklace; marked “sterling”. *1930s* ★★★★☆

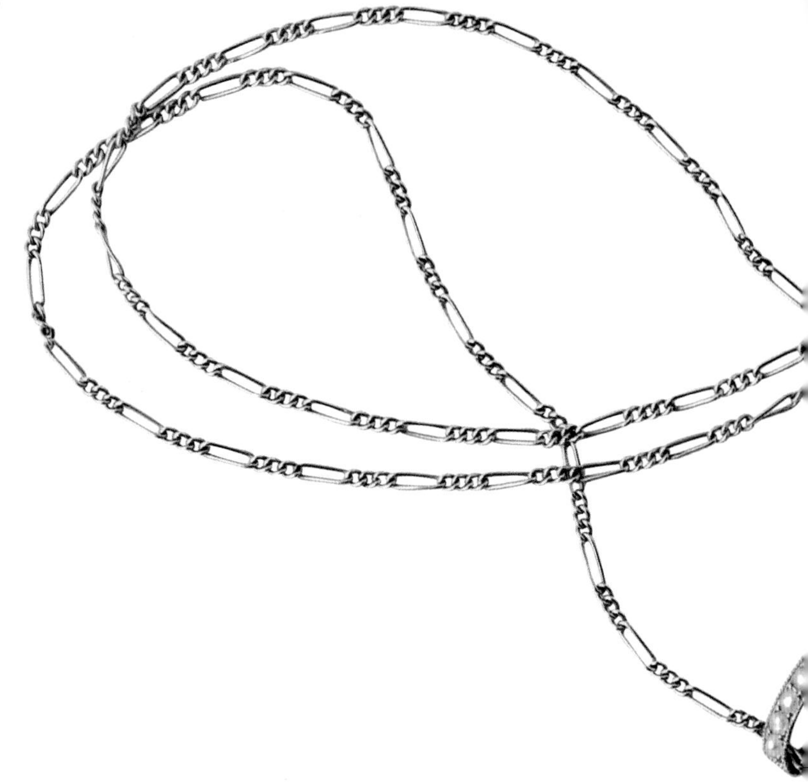

"I love vulgarity. Good taste is death, vulgarity is life."

MARY QUANT

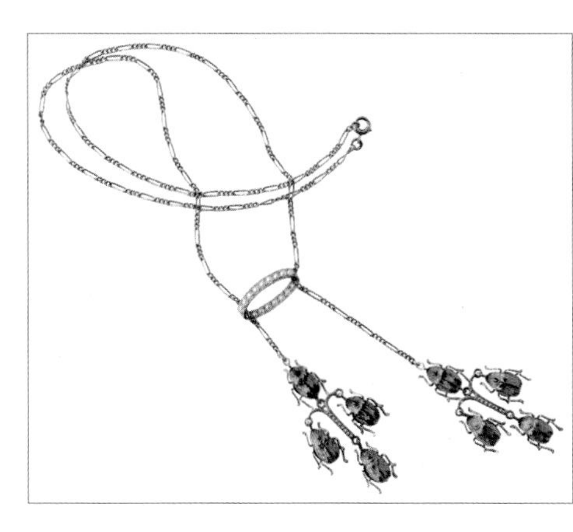

Gold twin-pendant necklace, each with a quartet of fluorescent blue beetles. *c.1900* ★★★★★

1950S RHINESTONE JEWELRY

Faceted glass and crystal stones have been used as a sparkling and affordable alternative to diamonds for more than two centuries. During the 1950s, consumer demand for rhinestones soared as women sought to copy the latest look of their favorite Hollywood stars. Ornate, glittering pieces were produced in a variety of styles and designs to complement every fashionable outfit and suit every pocket. At the top end of the market, Dior, Schiaparelli, and other great names in fashion designed high-quality pieces aimed at a wealthy clientele. More affordable versions were produced by companies such as Lisner, Corocraft, and Art. When buying vintage pieces today, remember that chipped or replaced rhinestones can affect the value of rhinestone jewelry.

Floral motif necklace with silvered metal links and round- and navette-cut *aurora borealis* rhinestones. *1950s* ★☆☆☆☆

English Art Deco necklace with triangular and shield-shaped sapphire blue-faceted glass stones. *Late 1920s* ★★☆☆☆

Austrian silver necklace set with clear crystal rhinestones and pendant polychrome glass beads. ★★★☆☆

French necklace with gilt metal chain links and multiple strands of faux pearls, polychrome glass stones, and beads. *1920s* ★★★★★

Faux coral woven bead necklace with two small rings inset with diamanté near the pendant. *1920s* ★★☆☆☆

Pair of shield-shaped earrings with asymmetrical faceted citrine and ruby colored glass, prong-set in white metal. *1960s* ★☆☆☆☆

Pair of earrings with citrine glass ovals, triangles, and clear crystal rhinestones. *1950s* ★☆☆☆☆

"Small circles glittering idly
in the moon,
Until they melted all into one track
Of sparkling light."

William Wordsworth

1960S ETHNIC JEWELRY

The increase in air transport during the 1960s led to a growth in foreign travel and an interest in exotic places around the globe. Exploration, whether in the outer reaches of space, faraway lands, or the workings of the mind, was a key theme of the decade and jewelers were inspired to experiment with designs from different cultures. The Indian subcontinent was a favorite source of style for designers. Pieces were modeled on the shapes of traditional Indian jewelry. The bright colors and heavy golds of Indian textiles influenced the use of colorful beads, while the rich architectural flourishes of temples and state buildings inspired ornate settings.

Pair of "Jewels of India" earrings with starburst drops, of silver-tone metal set with faux lapis, faux coral cabochons, and clear crystal rhinestones. *1960s* ★☆☆☆☆

Pair of pendant hoop earrings of black and red tortoiseshell with bands of gold inlay. *c.1880* ★★★★★

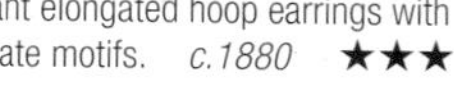

Pair of pendant elongated hoop earrings with inlaid gold floral and foliate motifs. *c.1880* ★★★★★

Pair of French earrings in gold-tone metal with green and white enameling, clear crystal rhinestones, and French jet cabochons. *1960s* ★☆☆☆☆

Pair of earrings with jet cabochons in filigree gold-plated metal. *c.1880* ★★☆☆☆

Pair of star motif earrings in silver set with bands of round-cut aquamarine crystal rhinestones. *1950s* ★☆☆☆☆

Leaf motif earrings in hand-beaten white metal with wire wraps. *1960s* ★★☆☆☆

"Will the people in the cheaper seats clap your hands? And the rest of you, if you'll just rattle your jewelry."

JOHN LENNON

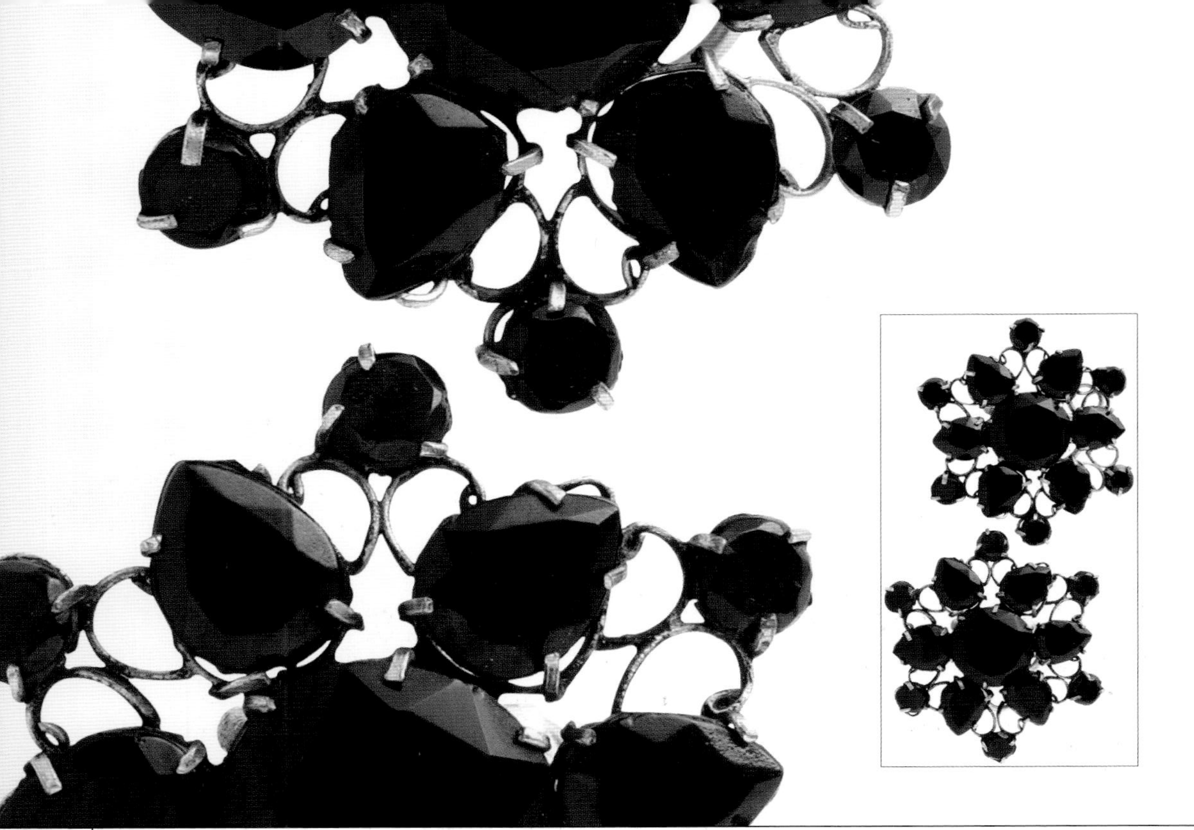

Georgian floral motif earrings of gold wire with round- and pear-cut French jet stones. *c.1720* ★★★★★

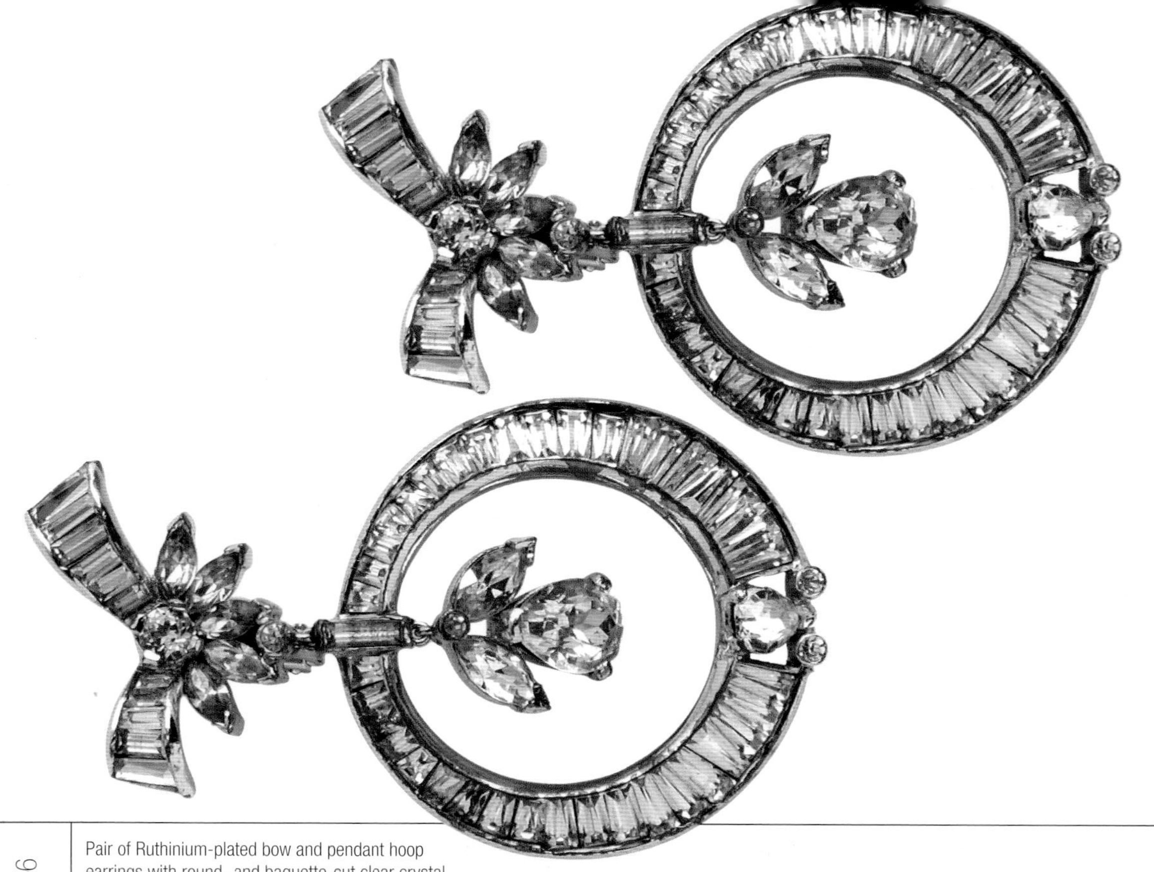

Pair of Ruthinium-plated bow and pendant hoop earrings with round- and baguette-cut clear crystal rhinestones. *1930s* ★★★☆☆

Pair of bow and pendant wreath earrings in silver with clear crystal rhinestones and a faux sapphire pendant center. *1920s* ★★★★★

Pair of pendant earrings with carved, shell-shaped, clear crystal drops. *1920s* ★★☆☆☆

BAKELITE

Bakelite is the catch-all term collectors use for plastic jewelry. Celluloid, which could be dyed to look like tortoiseshell or horn, was popular during the late 1890s, but was gradually eclipsed by Galalith and later by Bakelite. Patented in 1907 by Dr Leo Baekeland, Bakelite was tagged "the material of a thousand uses". Brightly colored and suitable for carving, it was adopted by jewelry designers from the 1920s to the 1940s. By the 1950s, Lucite, a clear plastic invented in 1937, had largely taken over in popularity. Bakelite "Philadelphia" bracelets and unusual novelty designs are among the most sought-after pieces of plastic jewelry.

Pair of carved Bakelite on carved wood dress clips, with a flower and leaf design. ★★☆☆☆

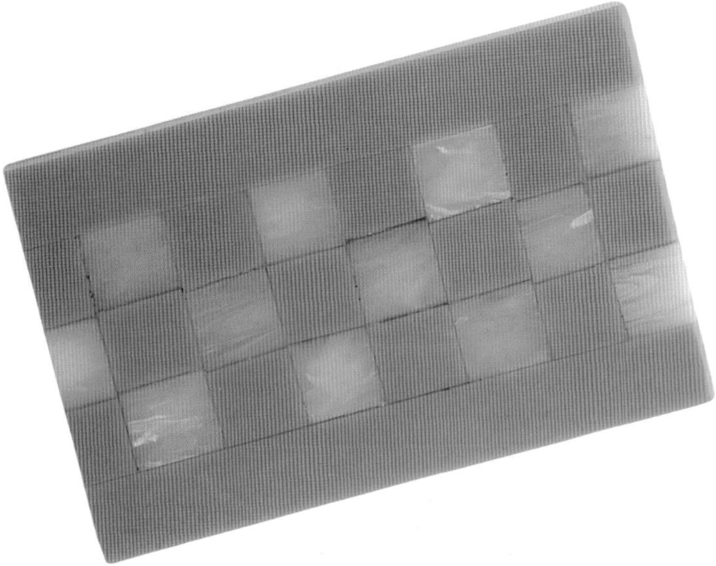

Luminous pink and gray checkerboard pin, possibly homemade. *1960s* ★★☆☆☆

Carved red Bakelite flower pin with five stylized curling petals. ★★☆☆☆

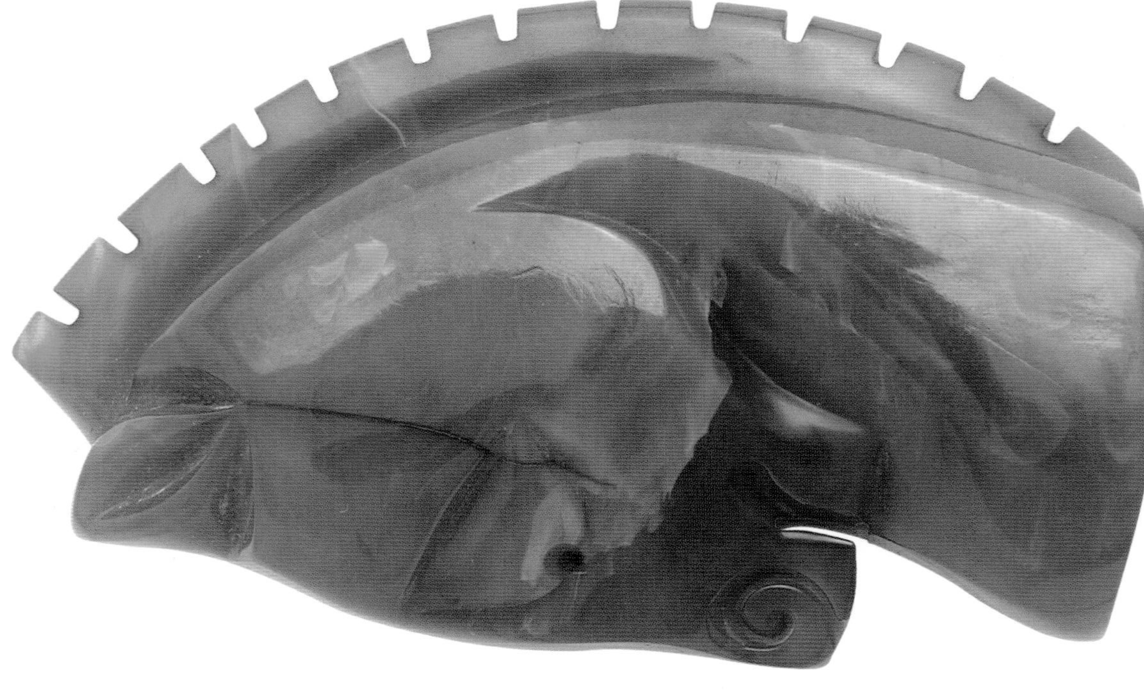

Carved marbled butterscotch pin in the shape of a chess horse. ★★☆☆☆

Burgundy round-eyed horse brooch with a fabric rope and metal harness and bridle. ★★★★☆

Rare wood on Bakelite gazelle pin. ★★★☆☆

Bakelite was carved using a rotating wheel to give beautifully smooth edges.

Carved and reverse-carved yellow Bakelite swan pin with a white painted background. ★★★☆☆

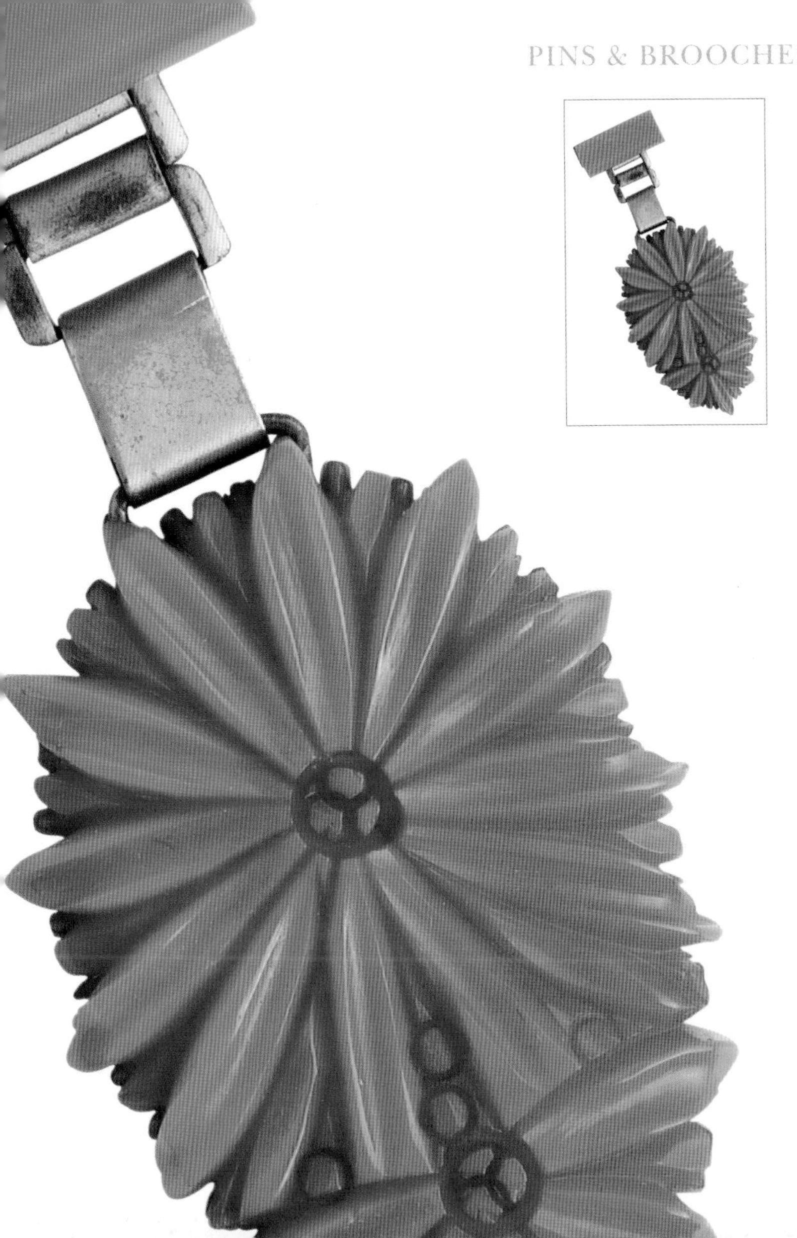

Carved orange Bakelite pin with an inverted teardrop-shaped pendant. *1930s–40s* ★★☆☆☆

Rare dangling pin, in a hunting theme, with horn, jockey's cap, boot, and metal-inlaid horseshoe. ★★★☆☆

Apple-juice colored Bakelite dangling fruit bar pin. ★★☆☆☆

Dangling Bakelite pins are much sought-after, especially when themed. Check for replacement parts and repairs.

Dangling cherries pin with green plastic leaves and plastic-covered string stems. ★★★☆☆

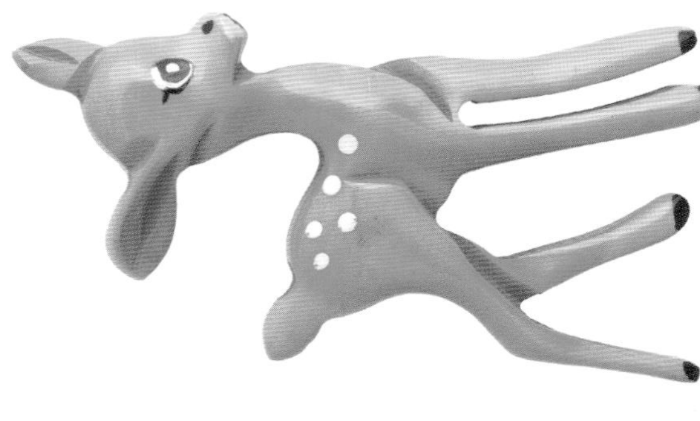

Painted corn colored "Bambi" pin with cream spots, probably made at the same time as the release of the 1942 Disney movie. ★★☆☆☆

Bakelite pineapple pin set on a wooden back carved as leaves. ★★☆☆☆

Black Bakelite was made to imitate jet. It was used to great effect to create striking geometric and stylized Art Deco designs.

Jet black carved swordfish pin with curved tail and incised gills. *1930s* ★★★☆☆

Carved and painted yellow Bakelite sword pin with painted black grip, covered with wire and pressed brass. ★★☆☆☆

"I love plastic. I want to be plastic."

ANDY WARHOL

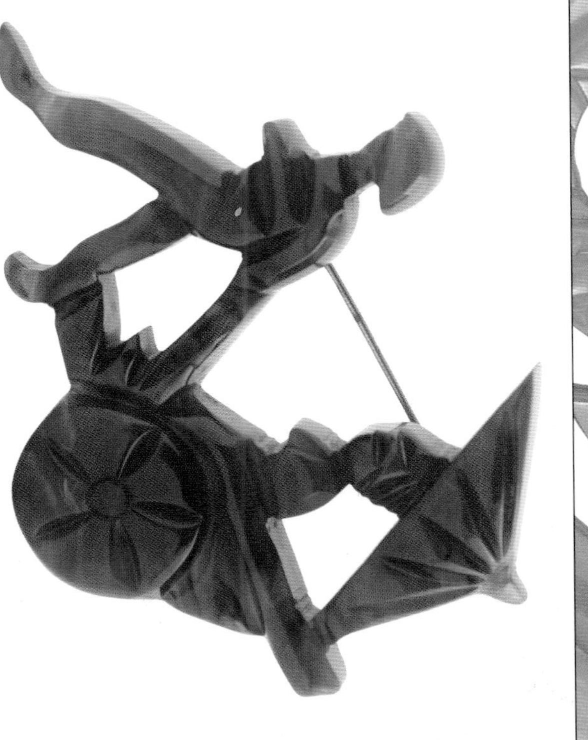

Chinese green Bakelite pin modeled as a man pulling a rickshaw. ★★☆☆☆

Large carved flower pin. The piece is almost as large as a bangle! ★★★☆☆

Known as the "material of a thousand uses", Bakelite was used to manufacture everything from telephones to the casing for World War II "bouncing" bombs.

Large and deeply handcarved cherry red leaf pin. ★★★★☆

Transparent tortoiseshell bar pin with a geometric carved pendant. ★★☆☆☆

The stylized heart shape has long been a symbol of love.

Red bleeding heart pin with cherries dangling from the center. *1940s* ★★★★☆

Bakelite novelty pin and chain modeled as a porter and suitcase, with highlights of gilt metal. *1930s* ★★★☆☆

"The things we truly love stay with us always, locked in our hearts as long as life remains."

Josephine Baker

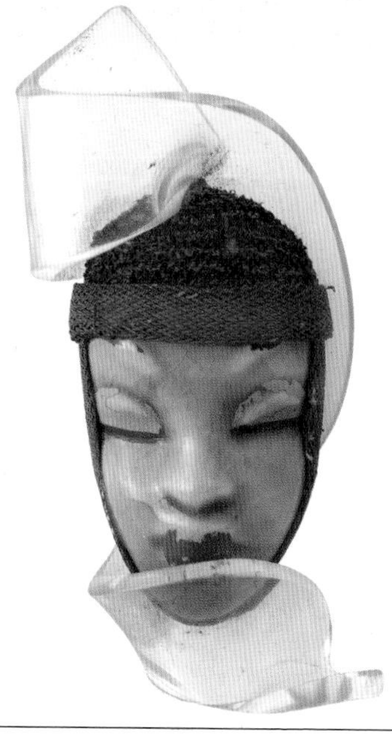

Painted porcelain and swirled Lucite pin named "Veiled Lady" by Elzac. The pin is modeled as Josephine Baker, the African-American singer and dancer. *1943* ★★★★☆

Burgundy handcarved flower and leaf oval pin. ★★☆☆☆

Large carved and painted Lucite pin modeled as the profile of a Native American, with painted details to the headdress. ★★☆☆☆

Deeply carved red Catalin pin with leaves and flowers. ★★★★★

Apple-juice colored Bakelite brooch with reverse-carved, painted, and filled details. *1930s* ★★☆☆☆

Double-knot pin in black Bakelite. The rhinestone highlights would have originally appeared clear, but now show as amber. *1920s–30s* ★☆☆☆☆

Reverse-carved and injected green Bakelite dress clips with oval flowers. ★★★☆☆

Schiaparelli-inspired Lucite and enameled "hand" pin, similar to a Chanel design. *1941* ★★★★★

Celluloid school-themed pin with dangling slate, book, and painted Bakelite pencil. *1930s–40s* ★☆☆☆☆

The craze for insect jewelry was started by the Victorians who were fascinated by natural history.

Large French Lucite cicada pin, painted on the outside and inside. *1950s* ★★★★☆

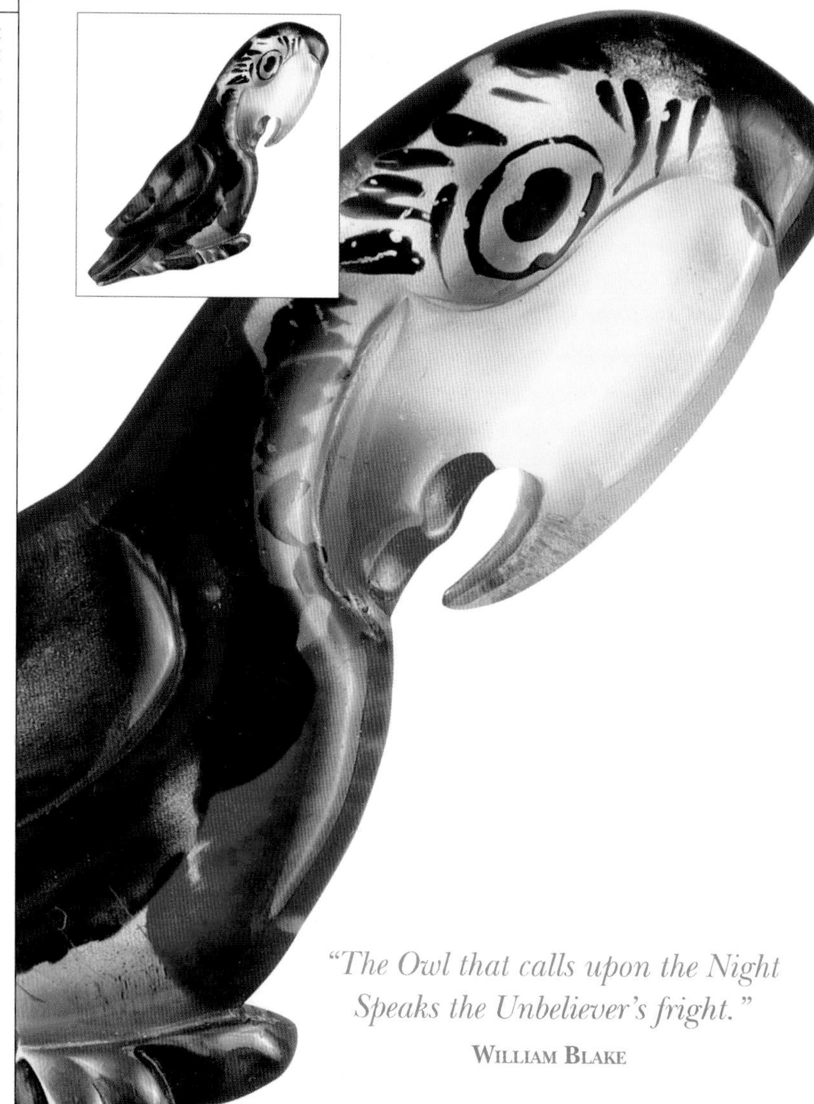

Multicolored Lucite parrot pin, with carved and painted detail, perched on a branch. *1930s* ★★☆☆☆

"The Owl that calls upon the Night
Speaks the Unbeliever's fright."

William Blake

Multicolored Lucite owl perched on a green branch pin, with carved and painted detail. *1930s* ★★☆☆☆

Art Deco African-style mask pin in black and red Bakelite with chromed steel eyebrows, nose, and mouth. *1920s* ★★★☆☆

African art and tribal masks had a powerful effect on Art Deco designers.

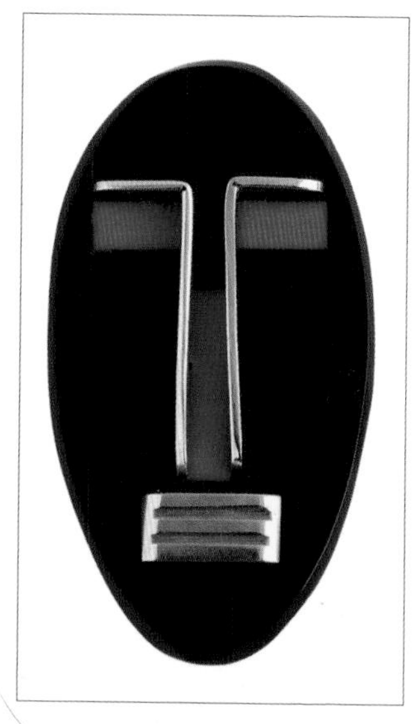

Italian flower pin with pale green brown Lucite petals and faux jet Lucite beads. *1980s* ★★☆☆☆

"At a flea market I always head for the junk jewelry table first."

ETHEL MERMAN

Plastic courting couple pin with revolving umbrella. *Late 1920s* ★☆☆☆☆

Quick to produce and reasonably priced, 1930s plastic jewelry appealed to customers in all income brackets.

Celluloid pin modeled as two bathing belles hiding behind a parasol. *Late 1920s.* ★☆☆☆☆

p.290
p.297
p.305
p.187
p.303
p.329
p.307
p.323
p.308

p.296 p.295 p.325

p.335 p.171 p.327

p.192 p.332 p.265

"PHILADELPHIA" BRACELETS

With their innovative design and brightly colored bands, "Philadelphia" bracelets are among the most sought-after types of Bakelite jewelry in the market today. The name is thought to date from 1985, when two bracelets in this style attracted unprecedented attention at a sale in Philadelphia. In 1998, a particularly fine example sold for $17,000, and similar bracelets in good condition regularly sell for several thousand dollars. A high level of workmanship was required in the manufacture of these bracelets. Each colored section had to be individually carved and then painstakingly fitted and glued together. The result is a striking geometric shape that is distinctly Art Deco.

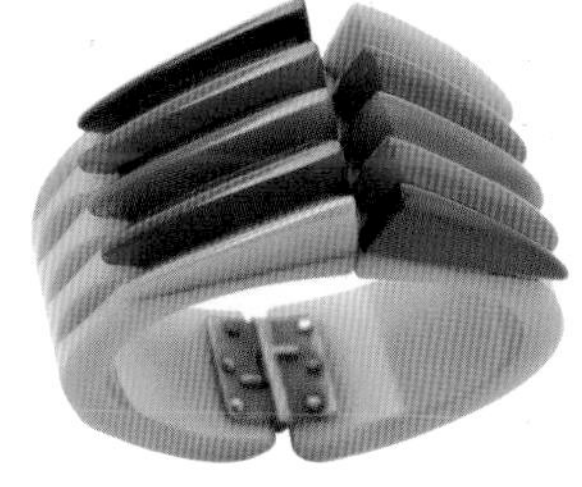

American "Philadelphia" hinged bracelet in red, green, black, and orange Bakelite. *1930s* ★★★★★

Red Bakelite riding-themed bracelet with brass insets; some elements have an overwash of color. ★★★☆☆

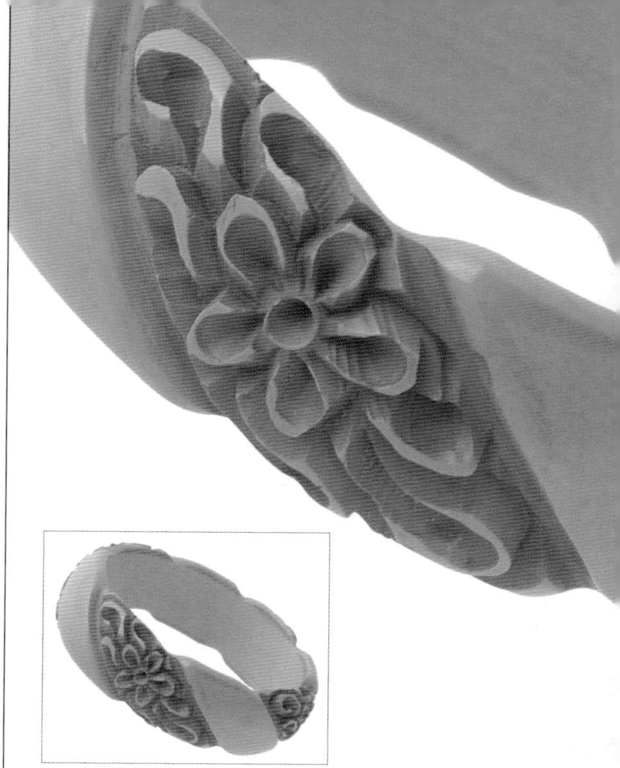

Yellow Bakelite bangle with diagonal plain and carved floral bands. ★★☆☆☆

"Philadelphia" laminated bracelet and matching earrings. ★★★★★

Heavily carved black articulated bracelet, in the Victorian style. ★★★★★

Handcarved green apple-juice colored bracelet. The color was injected late in the production process, and such pieces are very sensitive to temperature changes. ★★★★☆

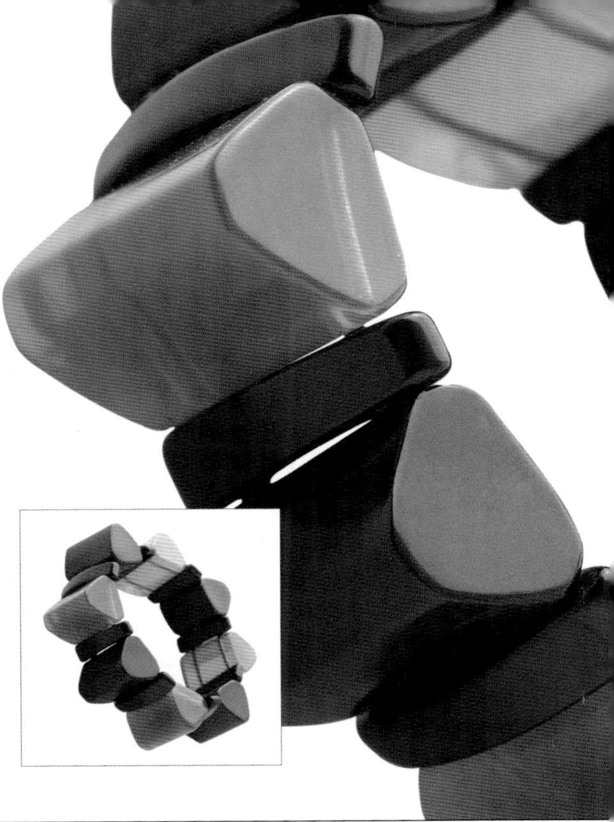

Art Deco apple-juice and black-colored elasticated bracelet. ★★★★☆

Apple-juice colored Bakelite bracelet with Czech glass and Egyptian styling. ★★☆☆☆

Chocolate brown Bakelite bracelet with razor-blade effect, from the Donald Alvin collection. *1940s* ★★★★☆

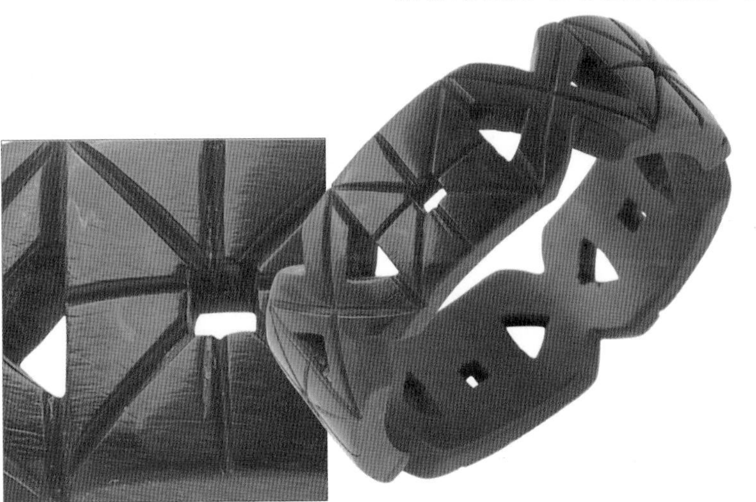

Heavily carved and pierced cherry red geometric bangle. ★★★★★

Heavily carved and pierced yellow flower bangle. *1930s* ★★★★☆

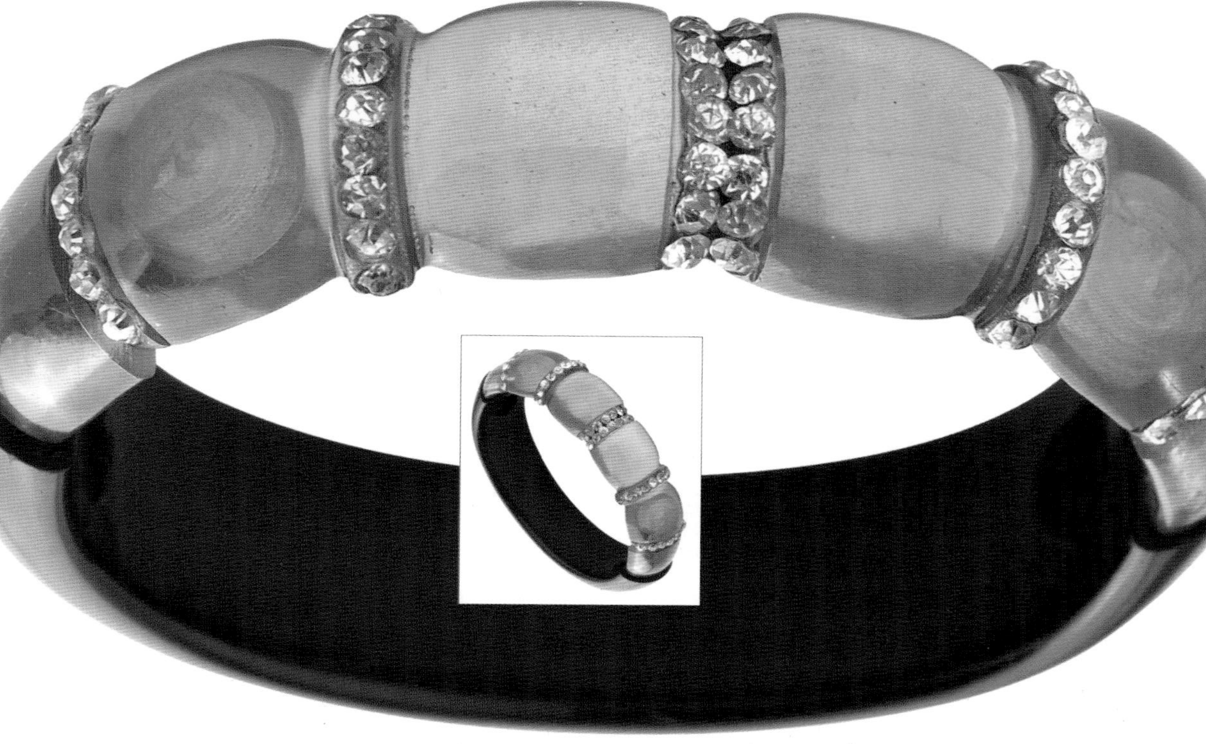

Apple-juice and black colored Bakelite and diamanté bangle. Such pieces combining different materials are much sought-after. *1940s* ★★★☆☆

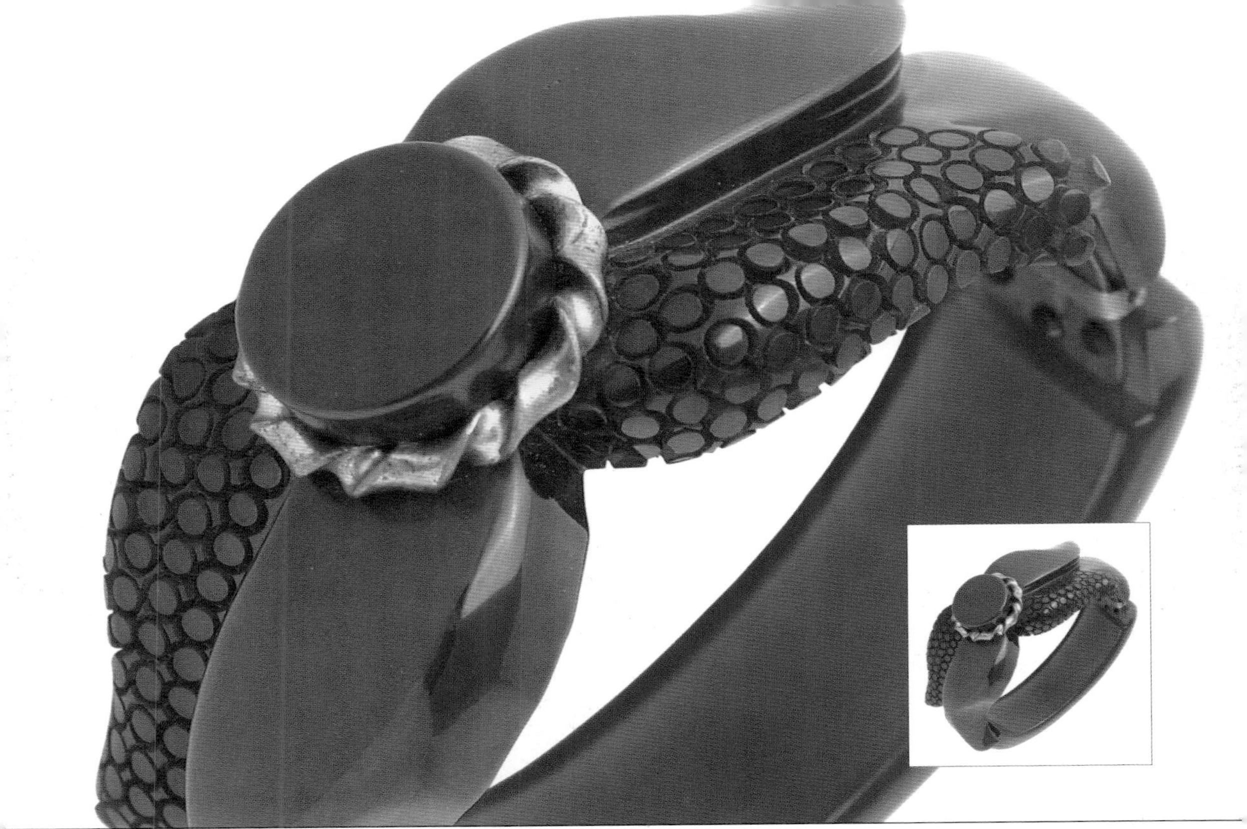

Black to translucent dark green hinged bracelet with gold-colored highlights. ★★★★☆

Coral colored Bakelite hinged bracelet with carved floral motif. ★★☆☆☆

"I was trying to make something hard, but then I thought I should make something that could be molded. That was how I came up with the first plastic – Bakelite."

Leo Baekeland

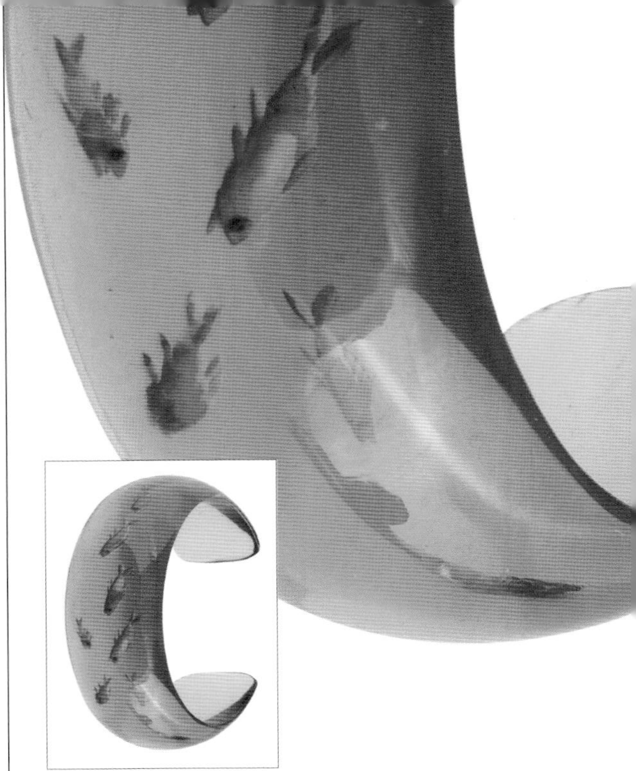

Large laminated yellow and black zig-zag bangle. ★★★★★

Apple-juice colored Bakelite cuff decorated with carved and painted fish. *1940s* ★★★★★

Black and ivory Bakelite snake bangle set with clear rhinestones and tiny brass beads. *1930s* ★☆☆☆☆

Handcarved green Bakelite bangle with inset daisy decoration. ★★☆☆☆

"Green is the key color of the world, and that from which its loveliness arises."

Pedro Calderon de la Barca

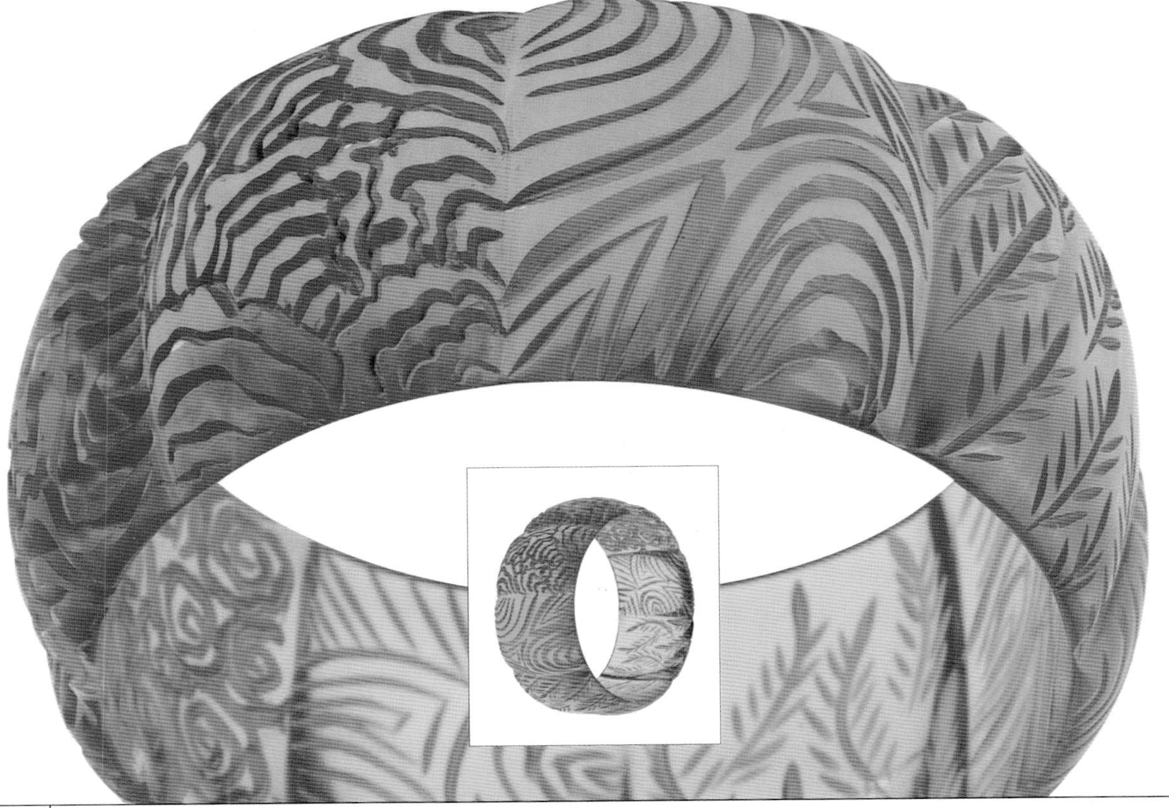

Reverse-carved apple-juice colored Bakelite bangle with eight floral and foliate-carved lobed sections. ★★☆☆☆

"Only great minds can afford a simple style."

STENDHAL

Art Deco celluloid bangle in the shape of a serpent, with diamanté details. *c.1930* ★☆☆☆☆

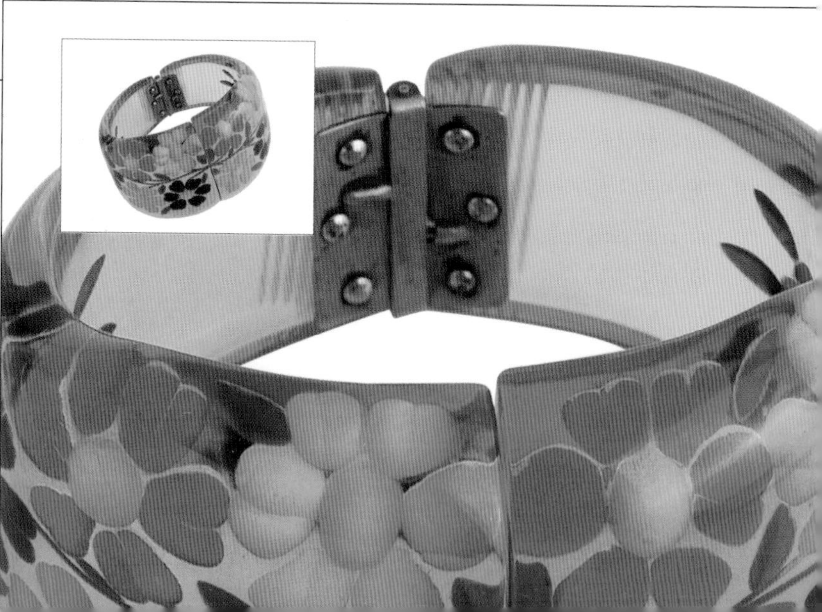

Apple-juice colored Lucite hinged bracelet with reverse-carved and painted flowers and foliage. *1930s* ★★★★☆

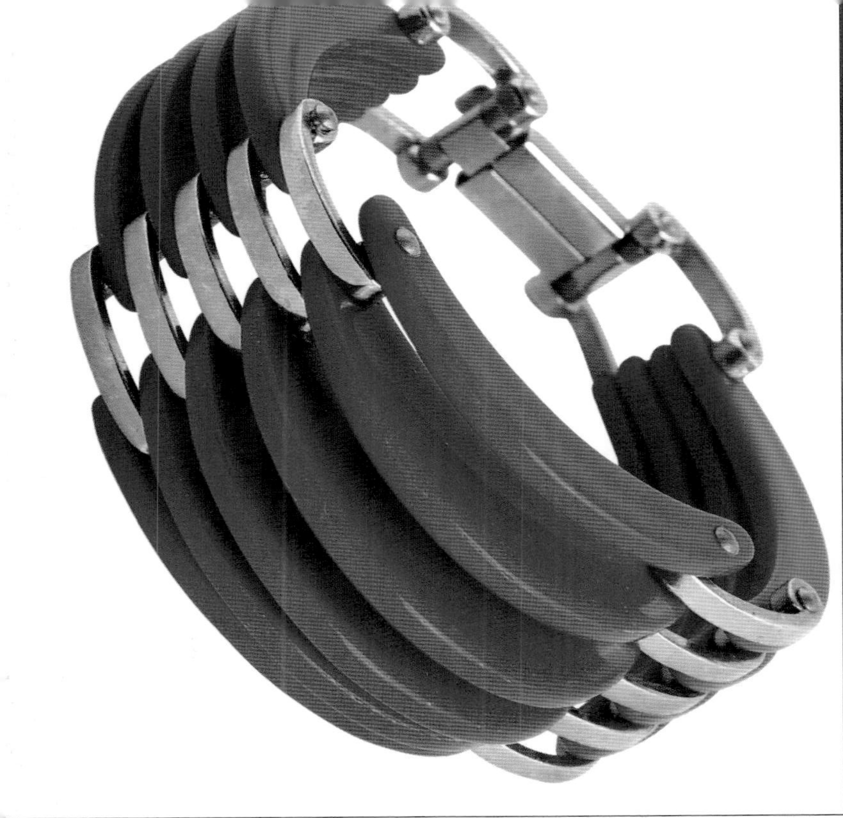

English Art Deco red Bakelite and chromed steel bracelet. *Late 1920s* ★★☆☆☆

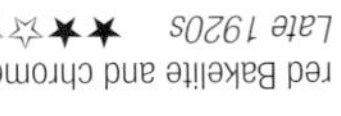

Pair of black and green clip earrings with an injection-molded green dot. *1960s* ★★☆☆☆

Pair of injected cream-in-brown Bakelite clip earrings. *1930s* ★★☆☆☆

Pair of green Bakelite cube earrings, each with three hanging chains supporting smaller cube drops. ★★☆☆☆

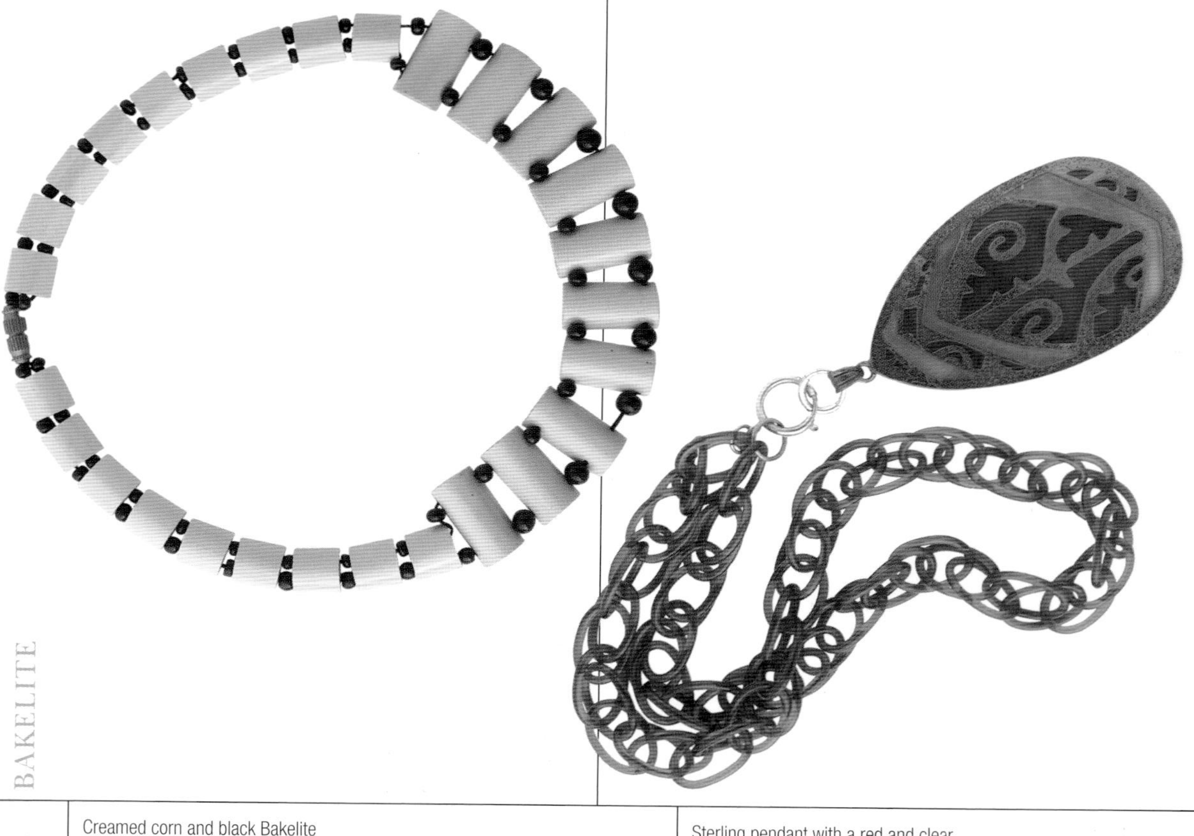

Creamed corn and black Bakelite articulated necklace. ★☆☆☆☆

Sterling pendant with a red and clear Bakelite chain. *1920s* ★★★★☆

Red and black cube necklace with a yellow chain. *1920s* ★★★★☆

Mottled orange and black Catalin pendant. The front swivels to reveal a mirror. ★★★★☆

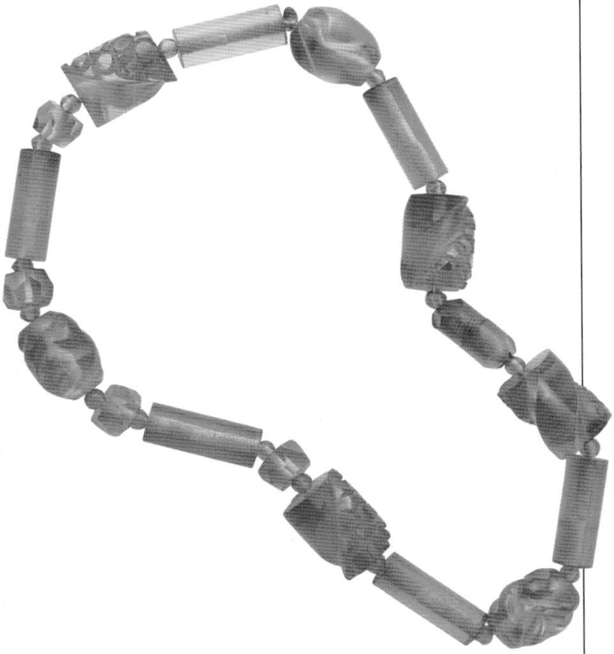

Handcarved apple-juice colored necklace with cylinder and dot parts. ★★★★☆

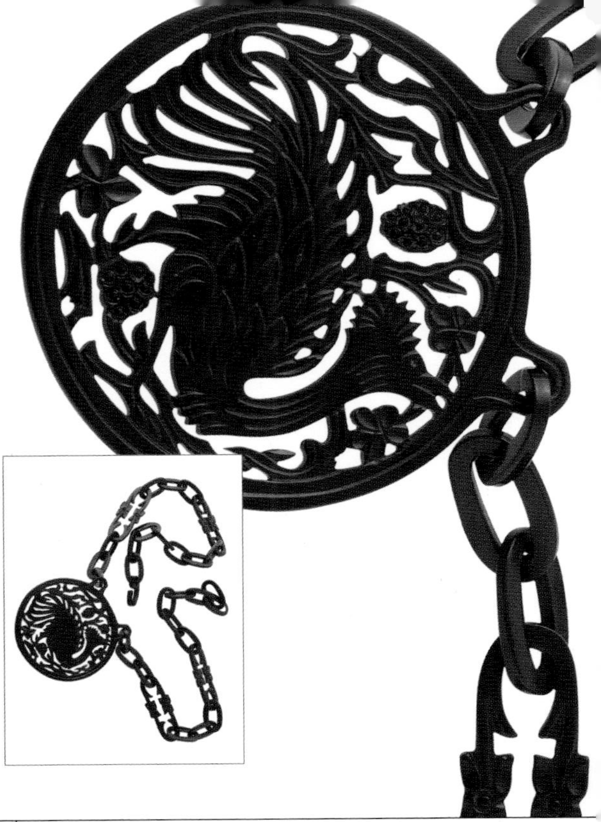

Black necklace with a handcarved peacock pendant. *1920s* ★★★★★

English Art Deco necklace with a silver chain and yellow and black Bakelite pendant. *Late 1920s* ★★☆☆☆

Look for pieces that are typical of the style of an era – such as Art Deco.

“Prystal” injected apple-juice and black colored Bakelite necklace, with reverse-carved decoration. *1930s* ★★★★☆

Green and beige carved necklace with metal fittings. ★★★☆☆

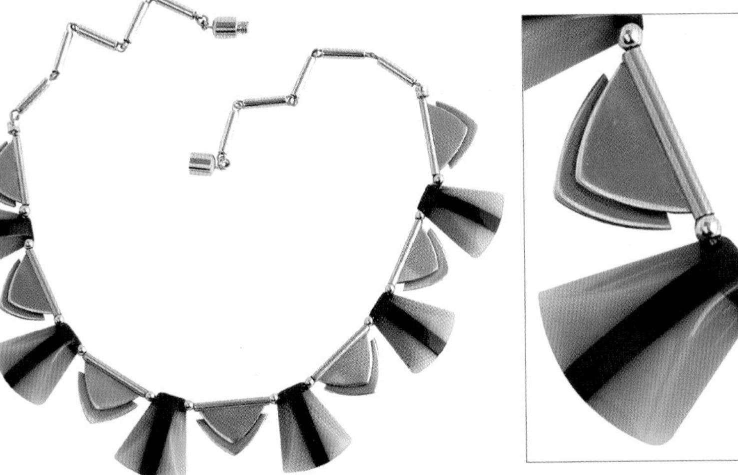

English Art Deco necklace: silver geometric forms alternate with green and black Bakelite. *Late 1920s* ★★☆☆☆

Donald Hedger two-tone Bakelite necklace in a geometric pattern. *1950s* ★★★★☆

"The only rule is don't be boring and dress cute wherever you go. Life is too short to blend in."

Paris Hilton

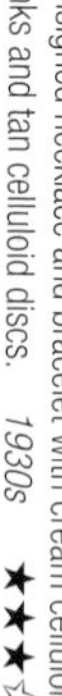

Unsigned necklace and bracelet with cream celluloid chain links and tan celluloid discs. *1930s* ★★★☆☆

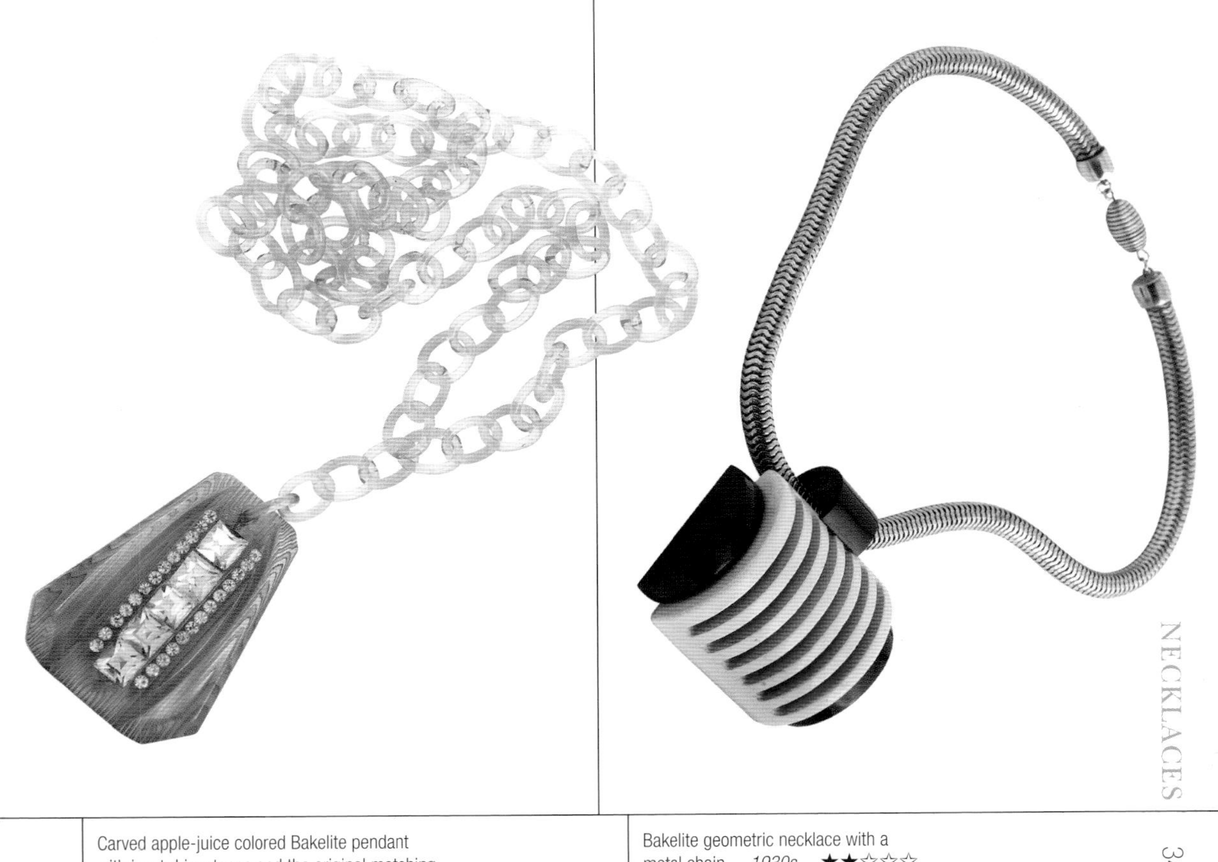

Carved apple-juice colored Bakelite pendant with inset rhinestones and the original matching necklace. *1930s* ★★☆☆☆

Bakelite geometric necklace with a metal chain. *1930s* ★★☆☆☆

Laminated brown and yellow striped square ring. ★★☆☆☆

Handcarved creamed corn-colored flower and triangle ring. ★☆☆☆☆

"Too much good taste can be boring."

Diana Vreeland

Green handcarved and stylized leaf ring. ★☆☆☆☆

HOT COLLECTING FIELDS

While some enthusiasts collect by designer or period, or simply choose pieces that complement their wardrobes, other jewelry fans collect by theme. Prices for popular costume jewelry themes have soared in recent years as the fashion for vintage jewelry continues to grow. Jelly Belly pins are particularly appealing. Unusual and cute, they have many devoted followers. Also popular are glitzy Christmas tree pins, produced by a variety of makers, and colorful Austrian fruit pins, made largely for the US market. Czech pieces also continue to attract a great deal of attention. Look out for pieces in good condition, made with high-quality materials, since these are likely to retain their value.

CHRISTMAS TREE PINS

Seasonal by design, stunning Christmas tree pins evoke the glitter and glamour of winter festivities. The tradition of wearing a decorative corsage in the holiday season dates back to the 19th century, when women adorned their dresses with pins made of ribbons, cloth, and trinkets. In the 1940s, metal jewelry in the shape of sleighs, wreaths, and most notably, Christmas trees, became popular. By 1950, mothers and wives were sending the Christmas tree pins to US servicemen fighting in Korea to remind them of life back home. The tradition stuck, and these pins, typically made from silver- or gold-tone metal and glass beads, are now a "hot" collecting area.

Lawrence Vrba Christmas tree pin in blue, ruby red, and clear crystal stones. ★★☆☆☆

"All that glisters is not gold;
Often have you heard that told."

WILLIAM SHAKESPEARE

Art pin of textured gilt metal with clear, red, green, and blue beads and rhinestones. *1950s* ★☆☆☆☆

French Bijoux Stern pin with green enamel and crystal rhinestones. *1980s* ★☆☆☆☆

Bijoux Stern pin in textured gold-tone metal with green and red enameling and multicolored crystal rhinestones. *1980s* ★☆☆☆☆

Cadora Christmas tree pin with cherubs and faux pearls. *1950s* ★☆☆☆☆

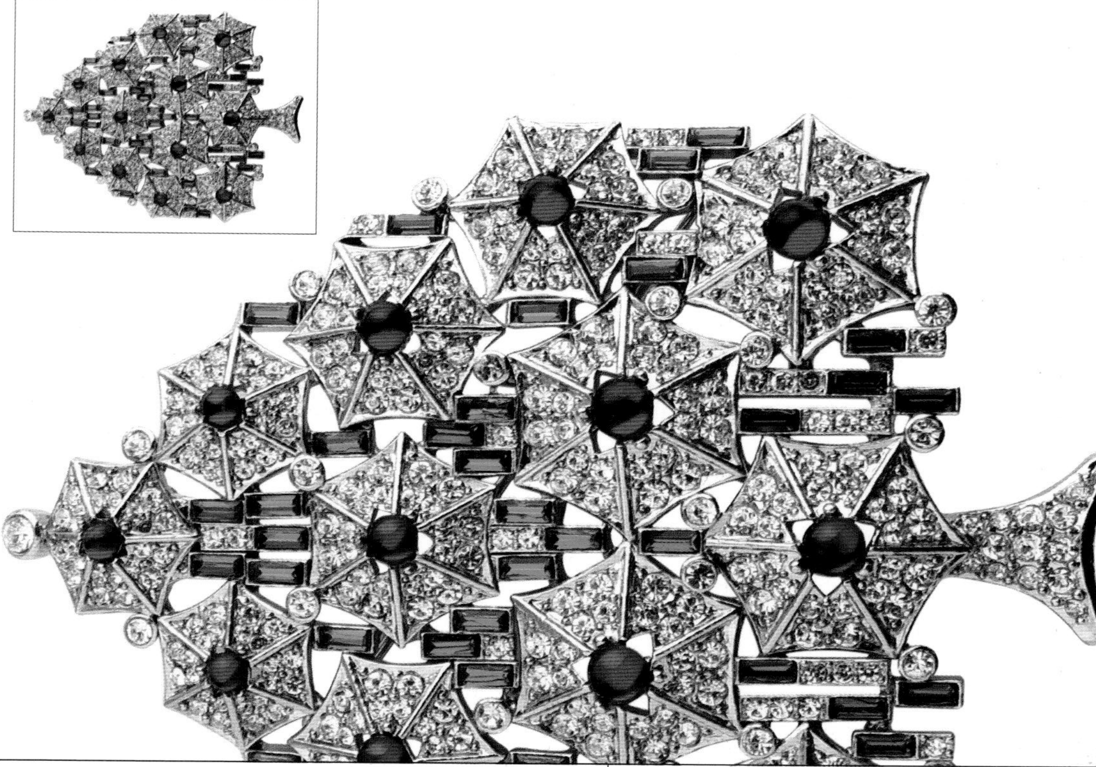

Cristobal Christmas tree pin set with ruby cabochons, green baguettes, and with diamanté flowers; one of a limited edition of 100. ★★☆☆☆

Only 300 trees of this style were produced, increasing their collectibility.

Cristobal Christmas tree pin set with red, amber, and green crystal rhinestones. *1999* ★★☆☆☆

Cristobal Christmas tree pin set with red, amber, and pale and dark green crystal rhinestones. *1999* ★★☆☆☆

Eisenberg Ice Christmas tree pin in textured gold-tone metal set with green, red, and clear crystal rhinestones. *1980s* ★☆☆☆☆

Eisenberg Ice Christmas tree pin in gold-tone textured metal set with *aurora borealis* and clear crystal rhinestones. *1980s* ★☆☆☆☆

Eisenberg Ice Christmas tree pin made of yellow-tone textured metal set with green enamel and multicolored crystal rhinestones. *1980s* ★☆☆☆☆

Eisenberg Ice Christmas tree pin in textured gold-tone metal set with green enamel and clear crystal rhinestones. *1980s* ★☆☆☆☆

"The perfect Christmas tree?
All Christmas trees
are perfect!"

CHARLES N. BARNARD

Lawrence Vrba pin with square-cut topaz Montana blue rhinestones. *1990s* ★★☆☆☆

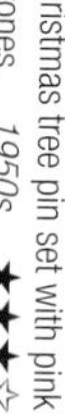

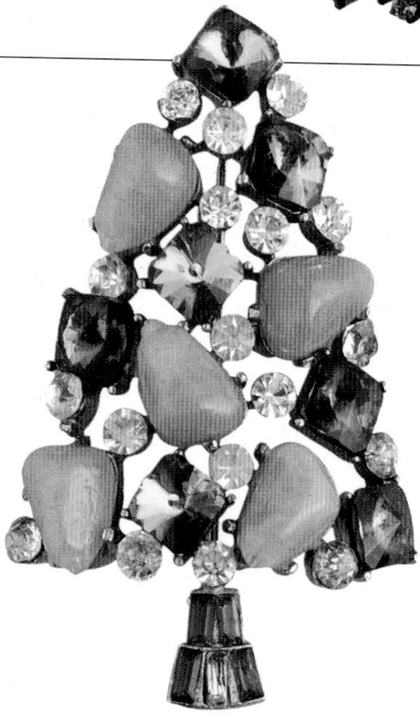

Mylu Christmas tree pin set with pink and green stones. *1950s* ★★★☆☆

English Sphinx Christmas tree pin with green enamel leaf and ruby red crystal rhinestones. *1960s* ★☆☆☆☆

Stanley Hagler pin with hand-wired green glass beads, red glass flowers, and crystal rhinestones. *1980s* ★★☆☆☆

Stanley Hagler pin with *aurora borealis* angel glass pendant, ruby red glass beads, and emeralds. *1980s* ★★☆☆☆

Stanley Hagler pin with frosted white glass flowers, hand-wired red crystal rhinestones, and red glass beads. *1980s* ★★☆☆☆

Stanley Hagler pin with hand-wired red glass beads, pearl bell flowers, green crystal rhinestones, and jadeite beads. *c.1990* ★★☆☆☆

Stanley Hagler pin with heart-shaped green glass stones, mother-of-pearl cabochons and bell flowers, and crystal rhinestones. *1980s* ★★☆☆☆

"He'd have given me
rolling lands,
Houses of marble,
and billowing farms,
Pearls to trickle
between my hands,
Smoldering rubies to circle
my arms."

DOROTHY PARKER

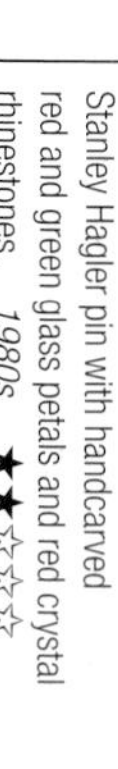

Stanley Hagler pin with handcarved red and green glass petals and red crystal rhinestones. *1980s* ★★☆☆☆

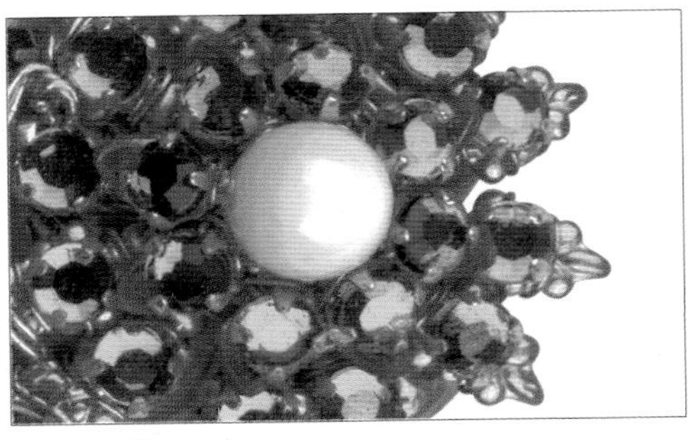

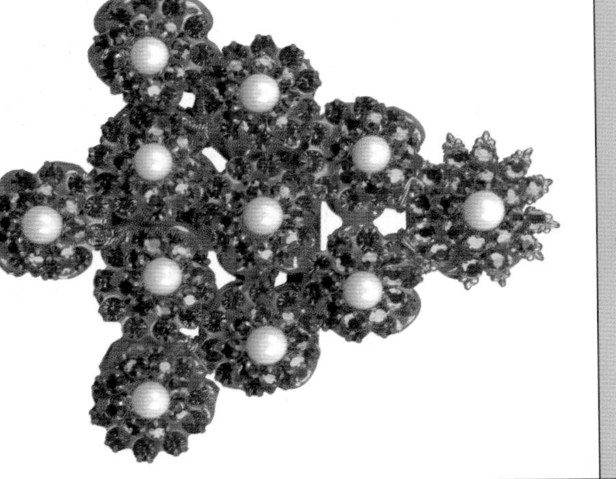

Stanley Hagler pin with opaque white glass beads and blue crystal rhinestones. *1980s* ★★☆☆☆

Stanley Hagler pin with molded opaque white glass stones, hand-wired green glass beads, and red crystal rhinestones. *1980s* ★★☆☆☆

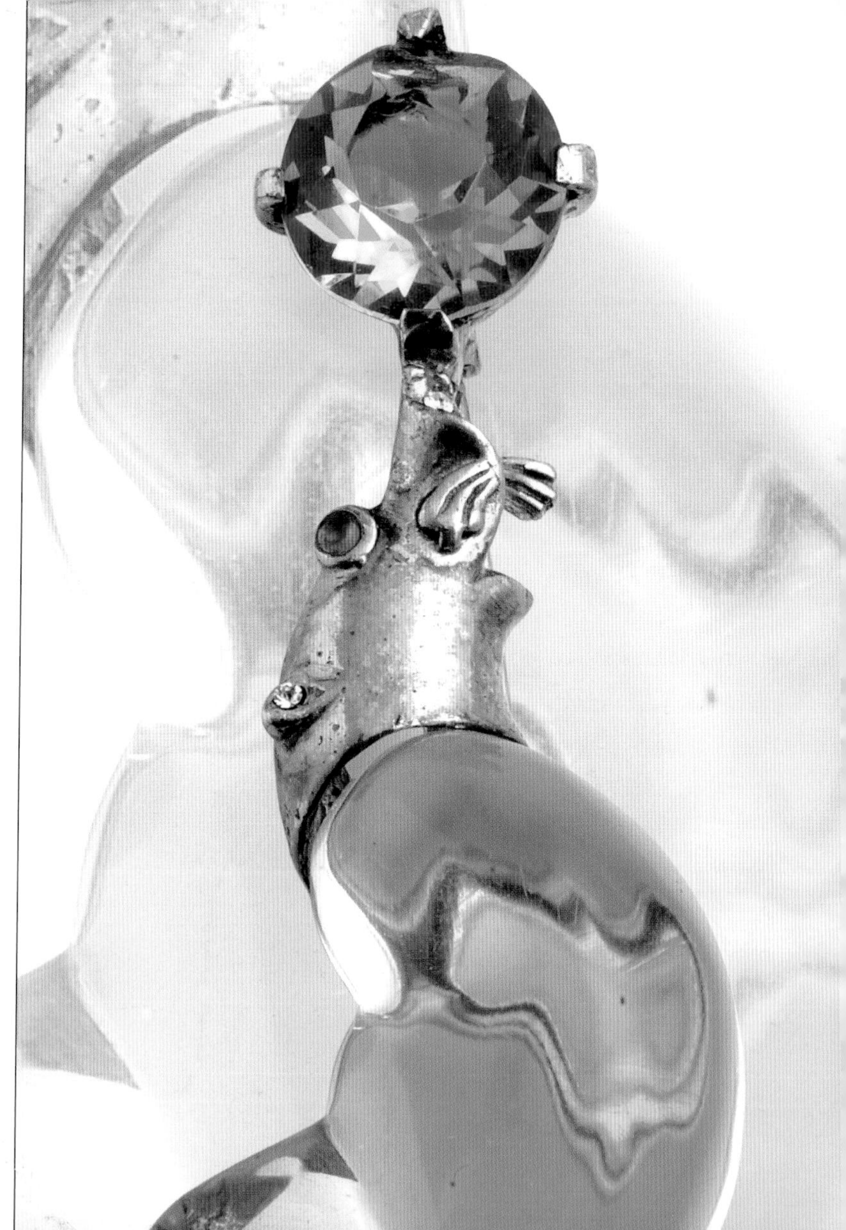

JELLY BELLIES

The diverse and imaginative jewelry of American maker Trifari has long been popular with followers of fashion and specialist collectors alike. Over the last few years, the company's famous "Jelly Belly" pins, originally designed by Alfred Philippe, have enjoyed increasingly high prices, particularly for pieces dating from the 1940s. The designs of other jewelry makers have also proved popular with collectors. Produced in a huge variety of adorable and unusual animal forms, from beetles and flies to dogs and chicks, each pin typically consists of a sterling-silver or gold-plated setting, clear rhinestone highlights, and a large central Lucite "belly". The value of each pin depends on its rarity and on the desirability of its form. Poodles, for example, are scarcer than roosters and so tend to attract greater interest.

Trifari Jelly Belly seal pin designed by Alfred Philippe, made of vermeil sterling silver with a clear Lucite belly, clear and ruby rhinestones, and a large prong-set sapphire rhinestone ball. *1940s* ★★★★☆

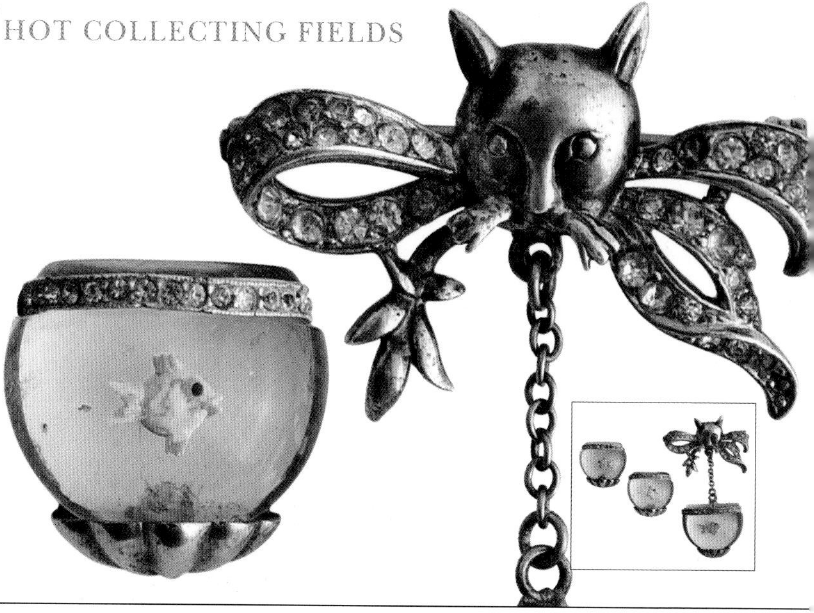

Very rare unsigned vermeil sterling-silver cat and Jelly Belly goldfish bowl pin and earring set, with clear crystal rhinestones and reverse-carved Lucite. *1940s* ★★★★★

Trifari Jelly Belly crab pin of vermeil sterling silver with a gray Lucite belly and clear rhinestone highlights. *1940s* ★★★★☆

American sterling-silver and gold-plated Jelly Belly penguin brooch with rhinestones and Lucite. *1940s* ★★☆☆☆

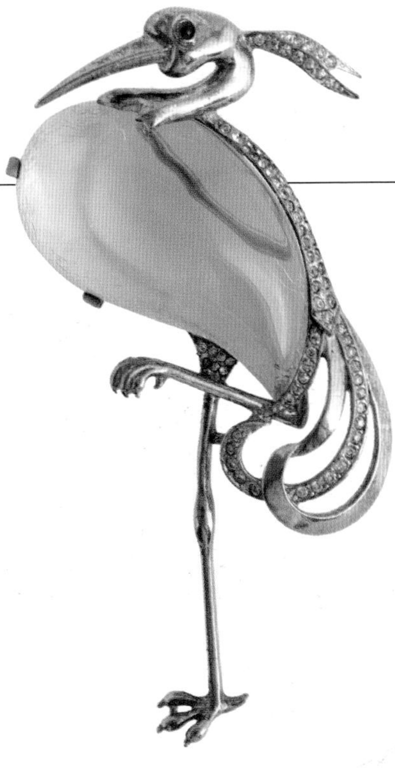

Invented in 1931, Lucite was used to make everything from war planes to purses.

Unsigned heron Jelly Belly pin in gold wash on silver, with a red cabochon eye and clear diamanté accents. *1940s* ★★★☆☆

Trifari Jelly Belly fly pin of vermeil sterling-silver, with a Lucite belly and clear rhinestones. *1940s* ★★★★★

Trifari Jelly Belly gold-plated chick-in-egg pin with a pavé-set clear rhinestone head and coral cabochon eyes. *1930s* ★★★★★

Creature pins are one of the most popular collecting areas.

Corocraft fish brooch designed by Adolph Katz, in sterling silver, enamel, and Lucite; signed "Corocraft Sterling America". *c.1945* ★★★☆☆

Trifari Jelly Belly gold-plated poodle pin with a clear Lucite belly and ruby red rhinestone eyes. *1940s* ★★★★★

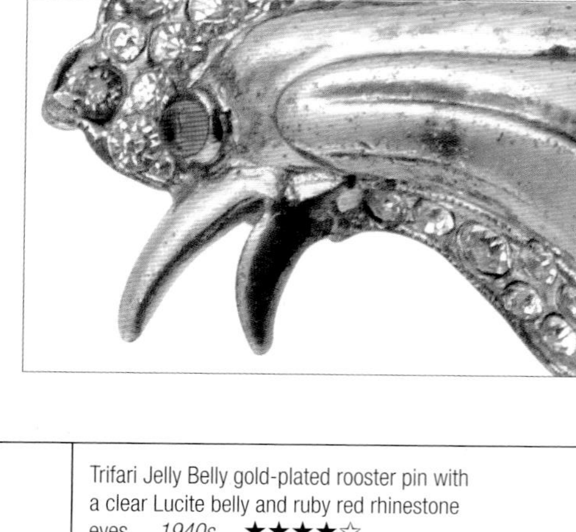

Trifari Jelly Belly gold-plated rooster pin with a clear Lucite belly and ruby red rhinestone eyes. *1940s* ★★★★☆

Coro Duette Jelly Belly pin by Corocraft studded with crystals. *1940s* ★☆☆☆☆

Unsigned Jelly Belly pin made with gold wash on white metal with a red cabochon eye and clear diamanté accents. *1950s* ★★☆☆☆

Unsigned Jelly Belly pin in the shape of a fish, with gold wash on white metal, a green cabochon eye, and clear diamanté accents. *1950s* ★★☆☆☆

AUSTRIAN FRUIT PINS

Juicy-looking fruit pins were made in Austria during the 1940s and 50s, almost exclusively for export to the United States. All marked "Austria", these colorful pins were manufactured in different factories throughout the country. Made of molded or carved glass with a clear or opaque finish, the most common motifs included strawberries, cherries, pears, and bunches of grapes. The glowing appearance of each fruit is enhanced by a backing of silver foil, making the bright colors appear richer and more light-reflective. Leaves and stems are typically fashioned from silver, gilt, or japanned metal. Enamel and crystal highlights are also found on some of the most attractive pins.

Red raspberries fruit pin with green leaves and a red diamanté highlight. *1950s* ★☆☆☆☆

Strawberry pin with red and amber glass, gold-plated leaf, and a rose pink crystal rhinestone highlight. *Early 1950s* ★★☆☆☆

Opaque red cherry fruit pin with green glass leaves and yellow diamanté. *1950s* ★☆☆☆☆

Large fruit pin with a single orange glass fruit and four green glass leaves. *1950s* ★☆☆☆☆

Fruit and leaf pin with gold-plated stems and with amber yellow and green glass fruit. *Late 1940s* ★★☆☆☆

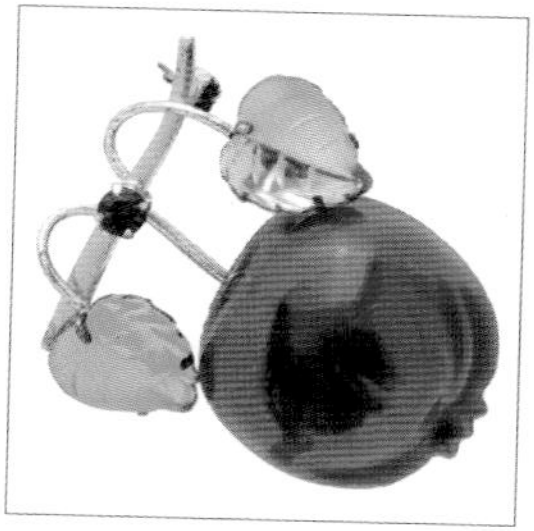

Pair of fruit pins in the shape of red raspberries with green leaves, and a red diamanté highlight. *Early 1950s* ★☆☆☆☆

Fruit pin in the form of a large red glass fruit, with two green glass leaves and a single center-set red diamanté. *1950s* ★☆☆☆☆

Opaque red cherry fruit pin with green glass leaves and a yellow diamanté highlight. *1950s* ★☆☆☆☆

Yellow glass single apple fruit pin with green glass leaves and a yellow diamanté. *1950s* ★☆☆☆☆

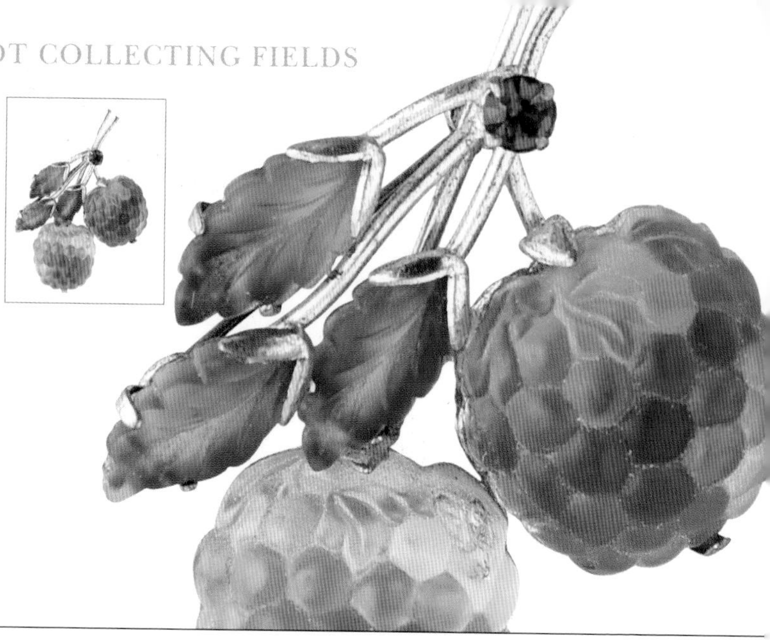

Fruit and leaf pin with a gold-plated stalk and with amber yellow and green glass. *Late 1940s* ★★☆☆☆

Red raspberries with green leaves fruit pin. *1950s* ★☆☆☆☆

"Life is just a bowl of cherries."

PROVERB

Black cherries pin and earrings set embedded with green leaves with a crystal rhinestone. *1950s* ★☆☆☆☆

CZECH PIECES

Czech craftsmen gained a reputation for quality and innovation when their colorful glass became the height of fashion during the late 19th century. It was not long before Czechoslovakian jewelry became equally popular. Production centered around northern regions of the country, particularly the towns of Harachov, Jablonec, and Liberec. Not surprisingly, makers took inspiration from the burgeoning glass industry and incorporated high-quality glass beads and crystal stones into their designs. Settings were produced by small local firms and were typically of yellow metal alloy, which was sometimes plated to appear as white metal. Today, Czech jewelry, particularly necklaces, is especially popular with collectors in the United States.

Multiple-pendant necklace of gilt metal with navette- and pear-cut sapphire blue rhinestones and a large, dark amethyst-colored cabochon. *Early 1900s* ★★☆☆☆

Heart-shaped pin with dark and light sapphire blue crystal rhinestones on a filigree blackened steel backing. *1940s* ★☆☆☆☆

Pin set with numerous crystal rhinestones of various cuts and gemstone colors in a filigree gilt metal backing. *Early 1900* ★☆☆☆☆

"Every generation laughs at the old fashions, but follows religiously the new."

HENRY DAVID THOREAU

Stylized floral motif pin with ruby, jade, amethyst, and sapphire crystal rhinestones set in a filigree gilt metal backing. *1940s* ★☆☆☆☆

Scrolled cartouche, triple-pendant pin of gilt metal with large, prong-set, Burmese-ruby colored oval cabochons. *1930s* ★★☆☆☆

Floral pin and earrings with aquamarine, amethyst, sapphire, emerald, and fuchsia crystal rhinestones, prong-set in a gilt metal casting. *c.1930* ★★☆☆☆

Long necklaces were especially popular with the "flappers" of the 1920s.

Czech necklace with a chain of silvered white metal and conical and tubular shaped pink beads, and with a pale pink oval glass cabochon and clear rhinestones pendant. *1920s* ★★☆☆☆

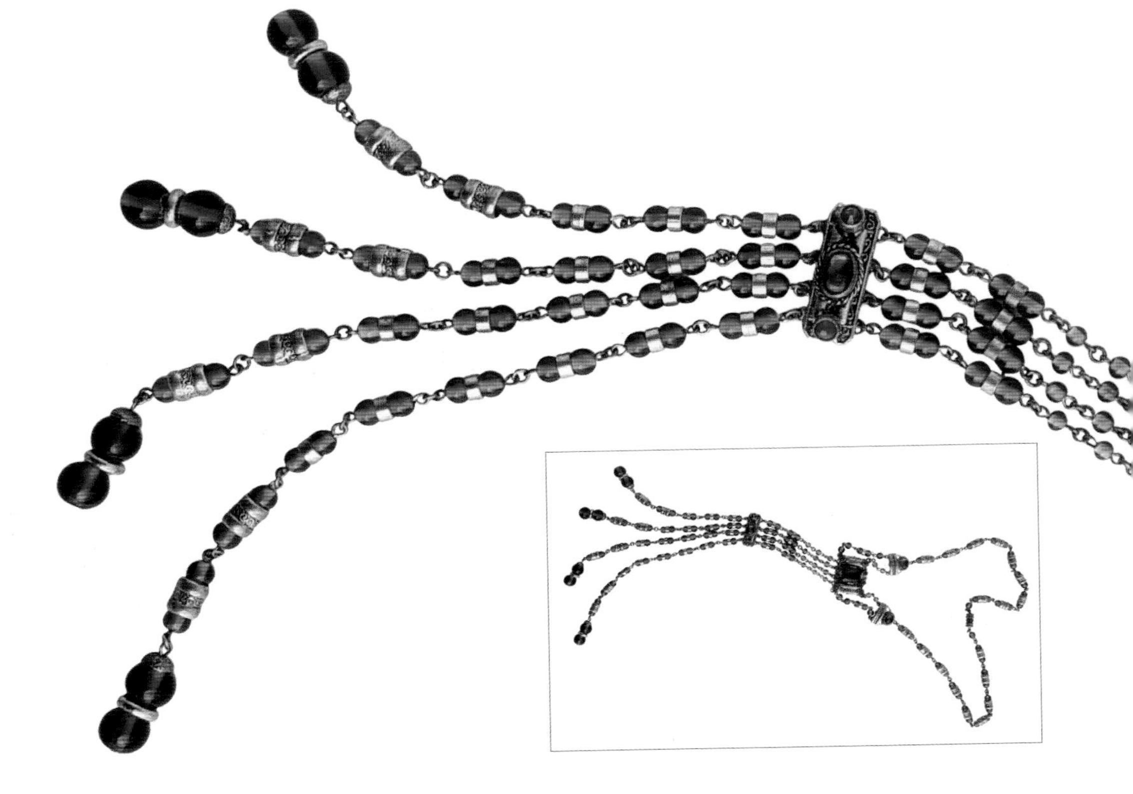

Quadruple-pendant necklace of gilt metal with round-, oval-, and square-cut red glass beads and stones. *1920s–30s* ★★☆☆☆

USING THE INTERNET

★ The internet has revolutionized the trading of collectibles as it provides a cost-effective way of buying and selling, away from the overheads of stores and auction rooms. Many millions of collectibles are offered for sale and traded daily, with sites varying from global online marketplaces such as eBay to specialist dealers' websites.

★ When searching online, remember that some people may not know how to accurately describe their item. General category searches, even though more time consuming, and even purposefully misspelling a name, can yield results. Also, if something looks too good to be true, it probably is. Using this book to get to know your market visually, so that you can tell the difference between a real bargain and something that sounds like one, is a good start.

★ As you will understand from buying this book, color photography is vital – look for online listings that include as many images as possible and check them carefully. Keep in mind that colors can appear differently, even between computer screens.

★ Always ask the vendor questions about the object, particularly regarding condition. If there is no image, or you want to see another aspect of the object – ask. Most sellers (private or trade) will want to realize the best price for their items so will be more than happy to help – if approached politely and sensibly.

★ As well as the "e-hammer" price, you will probably have to pay additional transactional fees such as packing, shipping, and possibly regional or national taxes. It is always best to ask for an estimate of these additional costs before leaving a bid. This will also help you tailor your bid as you will have an idea of the maximum price the item will cost if you are successful.

★ As well as the well-known online auction sites such as eBay, there is a host of other online resources for buying and selling, for example, fair and auction date listings.

MUSEUMS

CZECH REPUBLIC

Museum of Glass and Jewelry
U Muzea 398/4
Jablonec nad Nisou,
Libereck 466 01, Czech Republic
Tel: +420 483 369 011
www.msb-jablonec.cz

FRANCE

Musée Provencal Du Costume et du Bijou
2 rue Jean Ossola
06130 Grasse, France
Tel: +33 4 93 36 44 65
www.fragonard.com

Le Musée de la Mode et du Textiles
Union Centrale des Arts Décoratifs,
107-111 rue de Rivoli,
75001 Paris, France
Tel: +33 1 44 55 57 50
www.ucad.fr

ITALY

Il Museo del Bijoux di Casalmaggiore
Via A. Porzio, 9,
26-41 Casalmaggiore, Italy
Tel: +39 375 42309

RUSSIA

The Kremlin Museum
Moscow, Russia
Tel: +7 95 202 4256
www.kreml.ru

UK

Victoria and Albert Museum
South Kensington
London SW7 2RL, UK
Tel: +44 (0)20 7938 8500
www.vam.ac.uk

Ashmolean Museum
Beaumont Street,
Oxford OX1 2PH, UK
Tel: +44 (0)1865 278018
www.ashmol.ox.ac.uk

Birmingham Museum and Art Gallery
Chamberlain Square,
Birmingham B3 3DH, UK
Tel: +44 (0)121 303 2834
www.bmag.org.uk

Cheltenham Art Gallery and Museum
Clarence Street
Cheltenham
Gloucestershire GL50 3JT, UK
Tel: +44 (0)1242 237 431
www.cheltenhammuseum.org.uk

Liverpool Museum
William Brown Street,
Liverpool L3 8EN, UK
Tel: +44 (0)151 478 4399
www.liverpoolmuseums.org.uk

USA

The Metropolitan Museum of Art
1000 Fifth Avenue
New York, NY 10028-0198
Tel: 212 535 7710
www.metmuseum.org

Providence Museum of Jewelry
Office 4, Edward Street,
Providence, RI 02904
Tel: 401 274 0999
www.providencejewelrymuseum.com
By appointment only

DEALERS AND AUCTION HOUSES

Aurora Bijoux
USA
www.aurorabijoux.com

Barbara Blau
South Street Antiques Market, 615 South 6th Street,
Philadelphia, PA 19147-2128, USA
Tel: 215 739 4995
Tel: 215 592 0256
bbjools@msn.com

Bonny Yankauer
USA
bonnyy@aol.com

Charlotte Sayers FGA
313-315 Grays Antique Market, 58 Davies Street,
London W1Y 2LP, UK
Tel: +44 (0)20 7499 5478
sayers@grays.clara.net

Dawson & Nye Auctioneers & Appraisers
128 American Road,
Morris Plains, NJ 07950, USA
Tel: 973 984 6900
www.dawsons.org

Cristobal
26 Church Street,
London NW8 8EP, UK
Tel/Fax: +44 (0)20 7724 7230
www.cristobal.co.uk

The Design Gallery
5 The Green, Westerham,
Kent TN16 1AS, UK
Tel: +44 (0)1959 561 234
www.designgallery.co.uk

Eclectica
2 Charlton Place, Islington,
London N1 8AJ, UK
Tel: +44 (0)20 7226 5625
www.eclectica.biz

Eve Lickver
P.O. Box, 1778 San Marcos,
CA 92079, USA
Tel: 760 761 0868

Francesca Martire
Stand F131-137,
Alfie's Antiques Market
13-25 Church Street,
London NW8 0RH, UK
Tel: +44 (0)20 7724 4802
Cell phone: +44 (0)7990 523891
www.francescamartire.com

John Jesse
UK
By appointment
Cell phone: +44 (0)7767 497 880
jj@johnjesse.com
www.auctionsatcottees.co.uk

Junkyard Jeweler
USA
www.tias.com/stores/thejunkyardjeweler

Linda Bee
Grays Antique Market Mews,
1-7 Davies Street,
London W1Y 2LP, UK
Tel: +44 (0)20 7629 5921
www.graysantiques.com

Lynn & Brian Holmes
UK
By appointment
Tel: +44 (0)20 7368 6412

Mary Ann's Collectibles
South Street Antiques Center
615 South 6th Street,
Philadelphia, PA 19147-2128, USA
Tel: 215 592 0256
Tel: 215 923 3247

Marie Antiques
G107&136-137 Alfies Antique Market,
13 Church Street,
London NW8 8DT, UK
Tel: +44 20 7706 3727
www.marieantiques.co.uk

Mod-Girl
South Street Antiques Market, 615 South 6th Street,
Philadelphia, PA 19147-2128, USA
Tel: 215 592 0256

Million Dollar Babies
USA
Tel: 518 885 7397

Port Antiques Center
289 Main Street, Port Washington,
NY 11050, USA
Tel: 516 767 3313

RBR Group at Grays
158/168, Grays Antique Market, 58 Davies Street,
London W1K 5LP, UK
Tel: +44 (0)20 7629 4769

Rellick
8 Golborne Road,
London W10 5NW, UK
Tel: +44 (0)20 8962 0089

Richard Gibbon
UK
neljeweluk@aol.com

Ritzy
7 The Mall Antiques Arcade, 359 Upper Street,
London N1 0PD, UK
Tel: +44 (0)20 7704 0127

Roxanne Stuart
USA
Tel: 215 750 8868
gemfairy@aol.com

Sara Hughes Vintage Compacts, Antiques & Collectables
sara@sneak.freeserve.co.uk
http://mysite.wanadoo-members.co.uk/sara_compacts

Terry Rodgers & Melody
The Manhattan Art and Antiques Center
1050 2nd Avenue at 56th Street,
New York, NY 10022, USA
Tel: 212 758 3164
melodyjewelnyc@aol.com

Tony Moran
South Street Antiques Market,
615 South 6th Street, Philadelphia,
PA 19147-2128, USA
Tel: 215 592 0256

William Wain
Unit J6, Antiquarius, 135 King's Road,
London SW3 4PW, UK
Tel: +44 (0)20 7351 4905

INDEX

PICTURE CREDITS

The following images, photographed with permission from the sources itemized below are copyright © Judith Miller and Dorling Kindersley. (Abbreviations key: t=top, b=bottom).

Abacus Antiques p.224(t), p.308(b), p.332(t); **Aurora Bijoux** p.23, p.113(t), p.136(t), p.156(b), p.170, p.172(b), p.190(t), p.236(b), p.269; **Barbara Blau** p.151(t), p.152, p.170, p.178(b), p.254, p.290(b), p.295, p.308(t), p.311(t), p.336, p.337(t), p.338(t), p.347(t); **Baubles** p.166, p.175(t)(b), p.179(t), p.196, p.284; **Bonny Yankauer** p.12(t), p.13(b), p.14, p.15, p.15, p.55, p.137, p.146, p.167, p.208(t), p.209(t), p.210(t)(b), p.212(t), p.219(b), p.222(t)(b), p.223(t)(b), p.233(t), p.237(b), p.241(t), p.244, p.245(t), p.247(t), p.250, p.251, p.255, p.256, p.270(t), p.277(b), p.334(b), p.368(t), p.378(b), p.379(b), p.380(b), p.381(t)(b); **Chéz Burnette** p.131(t), p.136(b); **Cheryl Grandfield Private Collection** p.236(t); **Cristobal** p.13(t), p.18, p.21, p.22, p.24(t)(b), p.25(t)(b), p.27, p.35, p.40, p.42, p.43(t)(b), p.44, p.45(t)(b), p.46(t)(b), p.47(t)(b), p.50, p.53, p.56, p.57, p.60, p.62, p.64(b), p.65(t)(b), p.66(t)(b), p.67(t)(b), p.68(t), p.69, p.74, p.76(t)(b), p.77(t)(b), p.78(t)(b), p.79, p.80, p.81, p.82, p.83, p.84, p.85, p.86, p.87, p.88, p.89(t)(b), p.92(t)(b), p.93, p.94(t), p.95(t)(b), p.96(t)(b), p.97(b), p.98(t)(b), p.99(t)(b), p.100, p.101, p.102(t)(b), p.106, p.107, p.114(b), p.115(t), p.118, p.121(b), p.122, p.126, p.127(t)(b), p.130(t)(b), p.131(b), p.134(b), p.135(t), p.140, p.142, p.143(t), p.145(t)(b), p.147(t), p.149, p.150(t)(b), p.152, p.153(b), p.154, p.157(t)(b), p.158, p.160, p.162(t)(b), p.171(t)(b), p.172, p.173(t), p.179(b), p.180(t)(b), p.182, p.183(b), p.188(t), p.189, p.191, p.192(t)(b), p.195(b), p.204(t), p.209(b), p.211(t)(b), p.212(b), p.214, p.220, p.221, p.225(t), p.228(t)(b), p.230(t)(b), p.231(t), p.232(b), p.234, p.235, p.240(t)(b), p.241(b), p.243, p.246(b), p.249(t)(b), p.251, p.252(b), p.253(b), p.257, p.258(t), p.259(t)(b), p.262, p.268, p.279, p.280, p.283(t), p.284(t), p.286, p.315, p.352, p.354(t)(b), p.355(t), p.356, p.357(t)(b), p.358(t)(b), p.359(t)(b), p.360(t), p.361, p.362(t)(b), p.363(t)(b), p.364(t)(b), p.365(t)(b), p.366, p.369(b), p.372(t)(b), p.373, p.374, p.375, p.376, p.378(t), p.379(t), p.380(t), p.382(t)(b), p.383; **Charlotte Sayers FGA** p.233(t), p.267, p.268, p.269, p.271(b), p.285; **Dawson & Nye Auctioneers & Appraisers** p.330, p.333; **Eclectica** p.263(t)(b), p.264, p.265, p.266, p.274, p.276(t)(b), p.287(b), p.391; **Eve Lickver** p.290(t), p.291, p.292, p.293(t)(b), p.294, p.296(t)(b), p.297, p.298(t), p.299, p.300, p.301(t)(b), p.322(t)(b), p.332(b); **Francesca Martire** p.37; **Junkyard Jeweler** p.113(b), p.116 (t), p.320, p.143(b), p.190(b), p.195(t), p.202(b); **John Jesse** p.163, p.164, p.197, p.202, p.246(t), p.316, p.317, p.384, p.386(b), p.388; **Linda Bee** p.204(b), p.205, p.386(t), p.387; **Lynn & Brian Holmes** p.225(b), p.272, p.282(t)(b); **Mary Ann's Collectibles** p.184(t), p.346; **Marie Antiques** p.247(b); **Mod-Girl** p.61, p.64, p.112, p.128, p.148, p.173(b), p.176, p.178(t), p.185(t), p.232(t), p.298(b), p.303, p.304, p.305(t), p.306(t)(b), p.307(t)(b), p.308, p.309, p.310, p.311(b), p.323, p.324, p.325(t)(b), p.326(t)(b), p.327(t)(b), p.328, p.329, p.331(b), p.337(b), p.338(b), p.339, p.340, p.341(t)(b), p.343, p.344, p.345(b), p.348(t)(b), p.349; **Million Dollar Babies** p.115(b), p.156(t), p.165(b), p.202(t), p.203, p.253(t), p.389, p.390; **Port Antiques Center** p.347(b); **Private Collection** p.90, p.119, p.198, p.213, p.214, p.237(t), p.283(b), p.284(b); **RBR Group at Grays** p.135(b), p.252(t), p.258(b); Rellick p.193; **Richard Gibbon** p.30(t), p.32, p.36, p.68(b), p.70, p.71, p.103(b), p.120(t), p.129(t)(b), p.174(t), p.181(t), p.194(b), p.218(t)(b), p.219(t), p.224(b), p.226, p.231(b), p.255, p.267, p.270(b), p.271(t), p.369(t), p.371; **Ritzy** p.120(b), p.208(b), p.314, p.335, p.342, p.345(t); **Roxanne Stuart** p.20, p.26, p.34, p.97(t), p.103(t), p.104, p.118, p.132, p.141(b), p.144(t)(b), p.151(b), p.165(t), p.172(t), p.174(b), p.181(b), p.183(t), p.186, p.188(b), p.189, p.194(t), p.278, p.331(t), p.355(b), p.360(b); **Sue Mautner Costume** Jewellery p.12(t), p.17(t), p.44, p.48, p.49, p.52, p.54, p.58, p.116(b), p.117, p.141(t), p.159(t)(b), p.166; **The Design Gallery** p.248, p.334(t); **Tony Moran** p.305(b); **Terry Rodgers & Melody** p.94(b), p.134(t), p.147(b), p.153(t), p.184(b), p.185(b), p.215, p.229, p.245(b), p.277(t), p.278, p.287(t), p.312, p.313, p.368(b), p.370(t)(b); **William Wain** p.10, p.16, p.17(b), p.28, p.30(b), p.31(t)(b), p.33, p.59, p.114(t), p.121(t), p.124, p.125, p.266, p.273

ARCHIVE PICTURE ACKNOWLEDGMENTS

The publisher would like to thank the following for their kind permission to reproduce their material.

Golden Era Designers: Cristobal; **A–Z of Designers**: Lyon & Turnbull, 33 Broughton Place, Edinburgh EH1 3RR; **Unsigned Pieces**: Vin Mag Co, 39/43 Brewer Street, London, W1R 9UD; **Bakelite**: Swann Galleries Image Library, 104 East 25th Street, New York, New York 10010; **Hot Collecting Fields**: Decodame.com 853 Vanderbilt Beach Road, PMB 8, Naples, FL 34108

ACKNOWLEDGMENTS

AUTHOR'S ACKNOWLEDGMENTS

The Price Guide Company would like to thank the following for their contribution to the production of this book:

Photographer Graham Rae for his wonderful photography.

All of the dealers, auction houses, and private collectors for kindly allowing us to photograph their collections, especially Stephen Miners and Yai Thammachote at Cristobal, as well as Marion Barba, Linda Bee, Barbara Blau, and everyone at South Street Antiques Center, Richard Gibbon, Eve Lickver, Chrissie Painell, Melody Rodgers, Carol Spigner, Christopher St James, Jenny Stephens, Roxanne Stuart, William Wain, Liz Wilson, and Bonny Yankauer.

Also special thanks to Jessica Bishop, Julie Brooke, Mark Hill, Carolyn Malarkey, and Sara Sturgess for their editorial contribution and help with image sourcing.

Thanks also to Workflow Consultant Bob Bousfield.

PUBLISHER'S ACKNOWLEDGMENTS

Dorling Kindersley would like to thank the following for their contribution to the production of this book:

Claire Bowers and Richard Dabb for picture research, Caroline Hunt for proofreading, and Hilary Bird for indexing.